CW00377228

HAUTE SPACES

RESIDENCES

PAGE ONE

HAUTE SPACES: RESIDENCES

The cutting-edge interior designs featured in this series of books were selected from many talented designers worldwide. Particular attention was paid to the artistic styles of the interior elements including wall decorations, furnishings, lighting, colours, materials and textures. The outstanding interiors here are results of an artistic selection process.

This book is a must for designers and artists in interior design and architecture and contains high quality colour photos, floor plans, design concepts, and highlighted descriptions of outstanding elements which provide inspiration and technical understanding of each project.

HAUTE SPACES

Residences

• APARTMENT •

• LOFT •

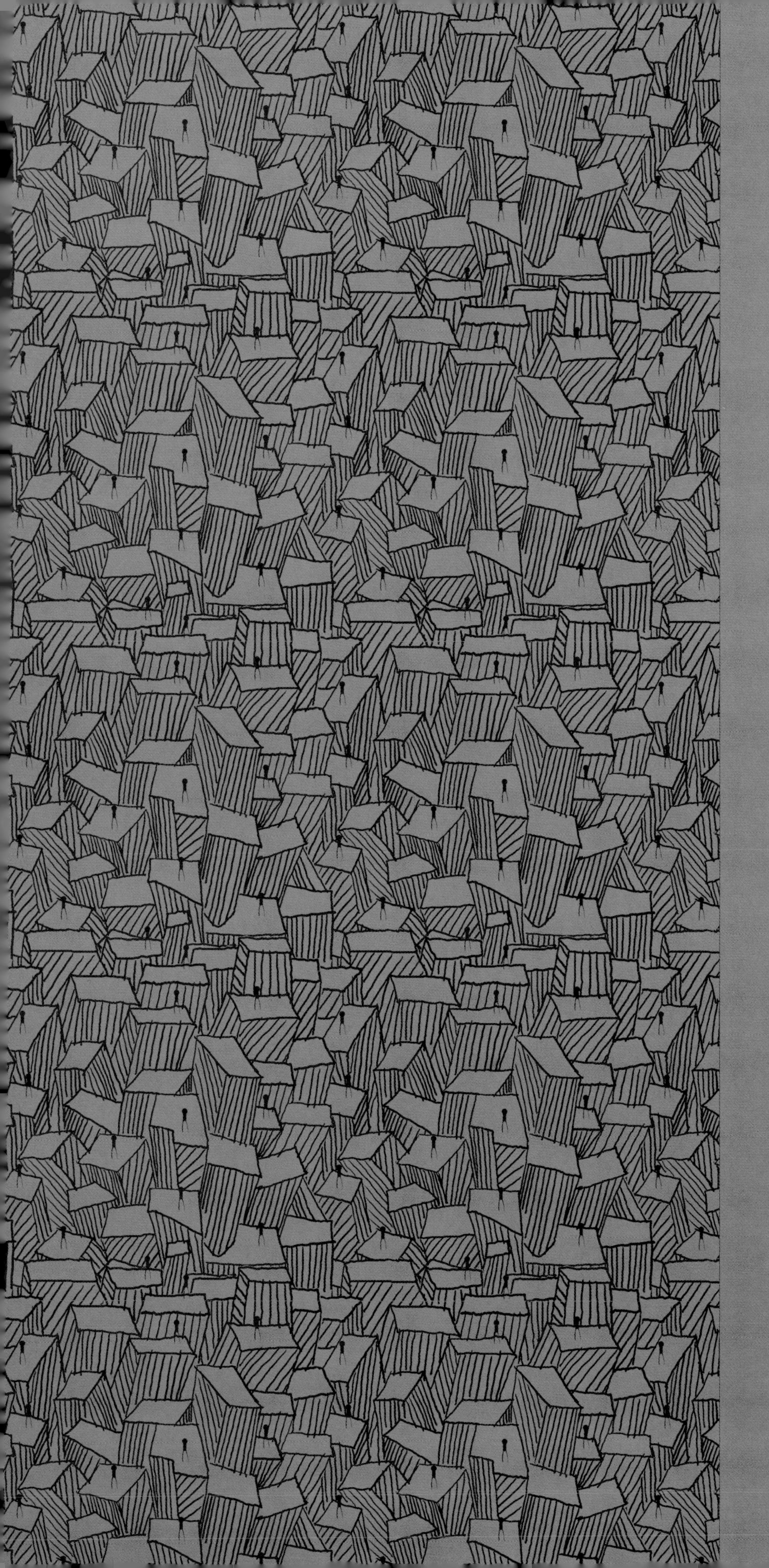

• VILLA + HOUSE •

HAUTE SPACES: RESIDENCES

The Book and All Seamless Patterns Created by Dopress (www.dopress.com).

008-123 APARTMENT
Haute Spaces: Residences

Apartment No.10

The apartment consists of rich artistic features, perfectly combining elegant retro charm with strong modern aesthetics. The living room floors and the hallway are of different materials but possess the same tone, which creates a variety in texture, form and colour. At the same time, they echo the sofa's linear patterns. The sculptures are crowning touch to this area's design, intensely enhancing the artistic atmosphere of the entire space.

The rich and varied textures are paid attention to in the design of the study. Textured walls and patterned carpets sharply contrast with the glossy curtains and furniture, making the collection and decorations on the shelves distinct.

The dining room and bedroom have similar ceilings with a metallic sheen under soft lighting, bringing about a beautiful atmosphere. Golden mosaic patterns on the wall of dining room harmoniously match with the leather chairs and carpet, as well as with the dark table and floor. This strongly reflects a style of luxury.

Name Of Project:
Apartment No.10
Location:
Shanghai, China
Completion Date:
2010
Interior Design:
Mohen Design International,
Hank M.Chao
Photography:
Mohen Design International,
Maoder Chou

Highlight: The apartment consists of rich artistic features, perfectly combining elegant retro charm with strong modern aesthetics.

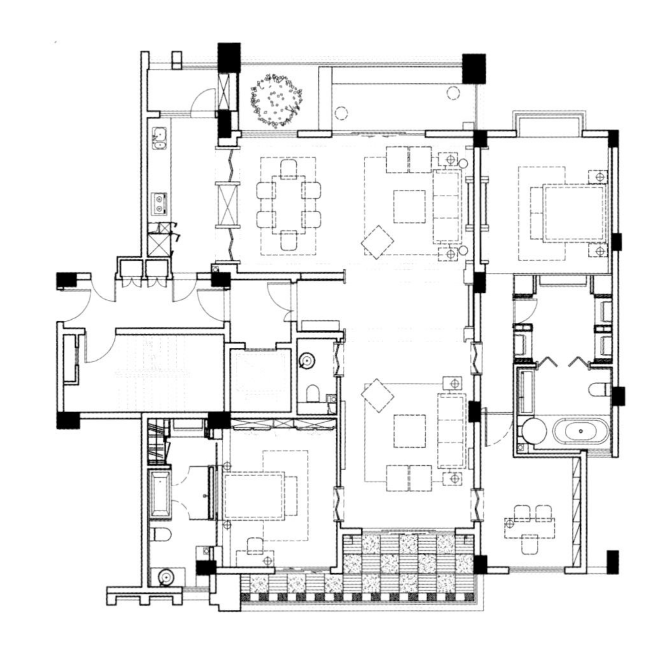

The mixed use of different materials that possess the same tone creates a variety in texture, form and colour. The sculptures are a crowning touch to this area's design, intensely enhancing the artistic atmosphere of the entire space.

Adria Showflat

Mere minutes away from Orchard Road, Adria apartments embody the sophisticated modernity of city life. They demonstrate simplicity at its best.

Monochromatic tones stylishly present each space within dark walls, contrasted against white Volakas marble flooring. Simple linear elements create interesting perspectives, while mirrors are cleverly employed to enhance the apartment's depth. Communal areas are compact yet luxurious with the fusion of kitchen, living and dining rooms. This seamless transition between areas gives the apartment an impression of greater space.

The kitchen is well appointed with simple yet elegant white cabinets resemble a clean, modern canvas. An interestingly layered bunk bed and glass study desk give the children's room an element of quirkiness, while a dramatic stone wall in the master bedroom serves as a key visual element.

Name of Project:
Adria 2-Bedroom Showflat
Location:
Singapore
Completion Date:
2010
Interior Design:
ONG&ONG Pte Ltd.
Lynn Ng
Photography:
See Chee Keong
Client:
Jumbo Valley Pte Ltd

Highlight: This work demonstrates simplicity at its best.

Monochromatic tones stylishly present each space within dark walls, contrasted against white Volakas marble flooring.

The Making of Your Home

Living Pod

This apartment is a new home to three youngsters in Hong Kong. Joey Ho Design has created an open and comfortable living pod which serves as a personal retreat away from the city.

To soften the sharp angles of the interior, Joey created a streamlined wall that wraps around the living space from the dining to the living area, and through to the foyer. This innovative framework conjures up a sense of an enclosure, creating a new spatial relationship for the interior, by organising it into various zones. A major design element of this apartment is the overlapping of spaces.

From living to dining room and bedroom, different layers and transparent materials intertwine both horizontally and vertically to create an open and cohesive spatial relationship the young people and the space. This enables them to embrace their new way of living.

Name of Project:
Living Pod
Location:
Hong Kong, China
Completion Date:
2008
Interior Design:
Joey Ho Design Ltd.
Mr. Joey Ho
Photography:
Mr. Graham Uden,
Mr. Ray Lau
Client:
Mr. Poon

Highlight: The Living Pod is open and comfortable.

The beautiful carpet with bright colours and round shapes not only responds to the streamlined wall, but also creates visual and tactile richness.

Meadows @Peirce

What makes the Meadows@Peirce duplex units unique is its seamless integration with nature and the smooth transition between activity and rest areas.

In this day and age, nature is a highly sought-after commodity that provides comfort from the burdens of modern city life. In this aspect, Meadows@Peirce is a haven with its 360 degree view of greenery. In addition, the first floor units of this condominium have their own private enclosed space of generous proportions, almost like a landed garden. The bedrooms have a distinguished consistency by similar timbre flooring, yet each room is unique in its layout and clever storage ideas. Ceiling-high bookshelves and quirky details blend effortlessly into the grid-like patterns of the walls and floors where clean, white marble creates an interesting harmony with the black-stained timbre flooring.

Meadows@Peirce embraces nature with its clean lines and liberal use of natural materials that brings city-dwellers back to the heart of nature.

Name of Project:
Meadows@Peirce
Location:
Singapore
Completion Date:
2010
Interior Design:
ONG&ONG Pte Ltd.,
Lynn Ng
Photography:
See Chee Keong
Client:
UOL Development Pte Ltd

Highlight: Meadows@Peirce is a haven with a 360 degree view of greenery that brings city-dwellers back to the heart of nature.

Ceiling-high bookshelves and quirky details blend effortlessly into the grid-like patterns of the walls and floors where clean, white marble creates an interesting harmony with the black-stained timbre flooring.

9
X
10
POSSIBLY MAYBE
POSSIBLY MAYBE
POSSIBLY MAYBE

Thomas Residence

Playing with volume and proportion, the body of the Thomas Residence traverses a series of delayed thresholds creating two or three main points of discovery within this single fronted Victorian terrace. These spatial rhythms are similarly overlaid and integrated with the change in language from period façade to the new intervention at the rear.

The small site required every last millimetre to be utilised, hence all the internal walls of the previous partially detached rear are pushed to the site boundaries, effectively fortifying the internal and external living areas and maximising the site's potential useable area. Within the open space at the rear of the residence, a series of architectural objects are dropped onto the virtually clean slate.

This series of specifically positioned yet seemingly random geometric forms dangle precariously over the drop in floor level (accommodating the fall of the site) and house different functional zones that delineate spaces within the main area.

Name of Project:
Thomas Residence
Location:
Australia
Completion Date:
2009
Interior Design:
Matt Gibson A+D
Photography:
Johnny Wheatley
Client:
Mr.Thomas

Highlight: Spatial rhythms are overlaid and integrated with the contrast of architectural styles.

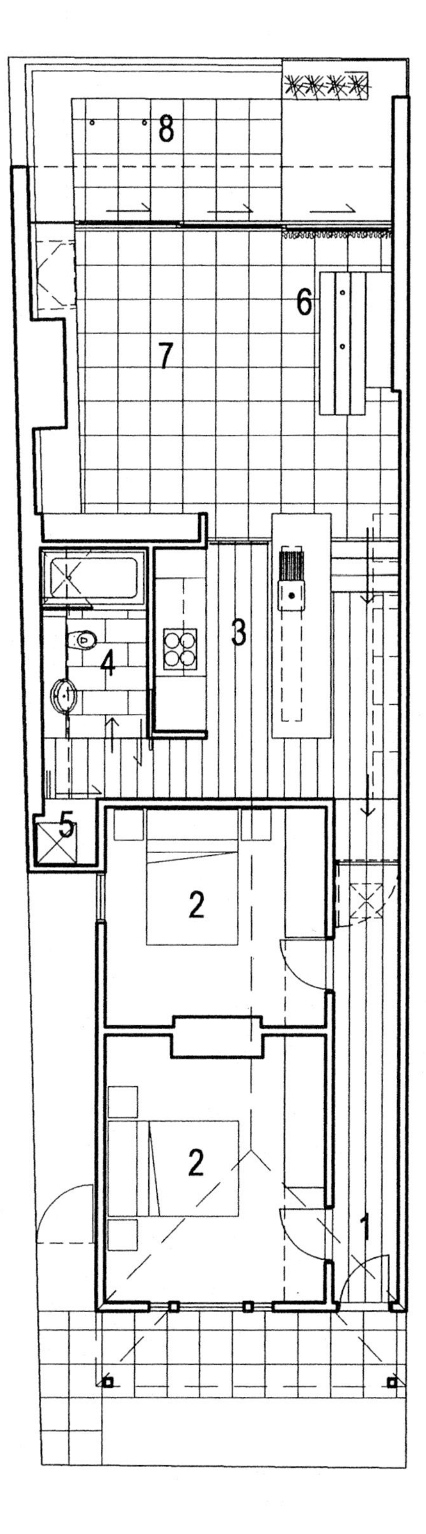

This series of specifically positioned yet seemingly random geometric forms dangle precariously over the drop in floor level (accommodating the fall of the site) and house different functional zones that delineate spaces within the main area.

Wuxi Apartment

Wuxi World Trade Centre Apartment is a masterpiece designed by PAL Design Consultants Ltd. This show flat situated on the CBD district aims to enhance traditional Chinese concepts with a contemporary approach to the apartment show in Wuxi.

To attract property clients, it was intended to represent luxury and quality infused traditional Chinese craftsmanship – all furniture was custom-designed with a mix of contemporary and antique styles. The show flat was divided into several functional areas such as the living, sleeping, leisure and study areas encompassed by screens with Chinese motifs.

Warm grey becomes a new conceptual colour to create a sense of richness, subtlety and harmony, being an aesthetic that reflects typical Chinese characteristics.

Name of Project:
Wuxi World Trade Centre Apartment
Location:
Wuxi, China
Completion Date:
2008
Interior Design:
P A L Design Consultants Ltd.,
Patrick Leung
Photography:
Bao Sze Wang
Client:
Wuxi World Trade Centre Co., Ltd

Highlight: The show flat highlights a traditional Chinese concept that employs a contemporary approach.

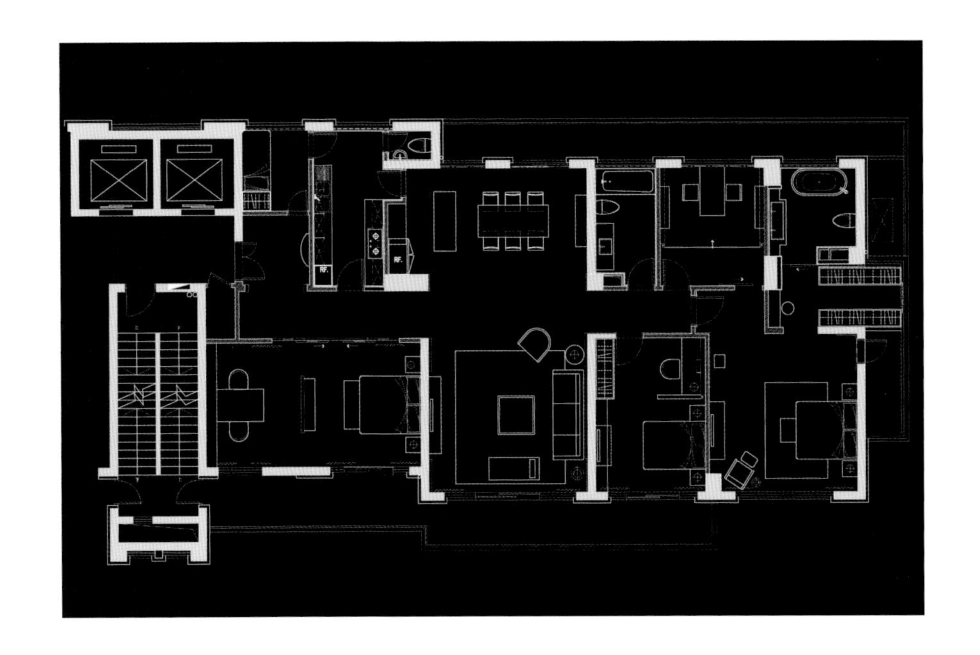

To integrate traditional Chinese craftsmanship, all furniture was custom-designed to be a mix of contemporary and antique styles.

White Residence

Before choosing the style and the architectural solution, the designers tried to get an insight into the client's character, preferences and her lifestyle needs in order to create a stylish, elegant, distinctive and feminine space. On the other hand, the architecture had to be strict and dynamic – just like the owner.

Therefore, the architectural solution applied was minimalistic with clear, regular lines and strict layouts, while décor was a synthesis of several styles. The interior includes vintage accessories, modern and Neo-baroque furniture, retro 1960s elements, a sculpture panel of an ancient arch, and high-tech materials and technology such as glass with diode illumination. The predominant colour of the interior is white, with lavender and chocolate for added visual effect.

Metalised wallpaper in the hallway is succeeded by velvety wall surfaces in the lounge and in the bedroom. An important component of the design was the installation of several lighting modes. In the daytimes sufficient amount of light comes through panoramic windows, while in the evening, special lighting including diode illumination transforms the apartment into a club while retaining a relaxed atmosphere.

Name of Project:
White Residence
Location:
Riga, Latvia
Completion Date:
2008
Interior Design:
Serge Serpuhov,
Dmitry Yukhnevich
Photography:
Martin Kudrjavcev
Client:
A Young Girl

Highlight: The architectural solution is minimalistic – clear, regular lines and strict layout.

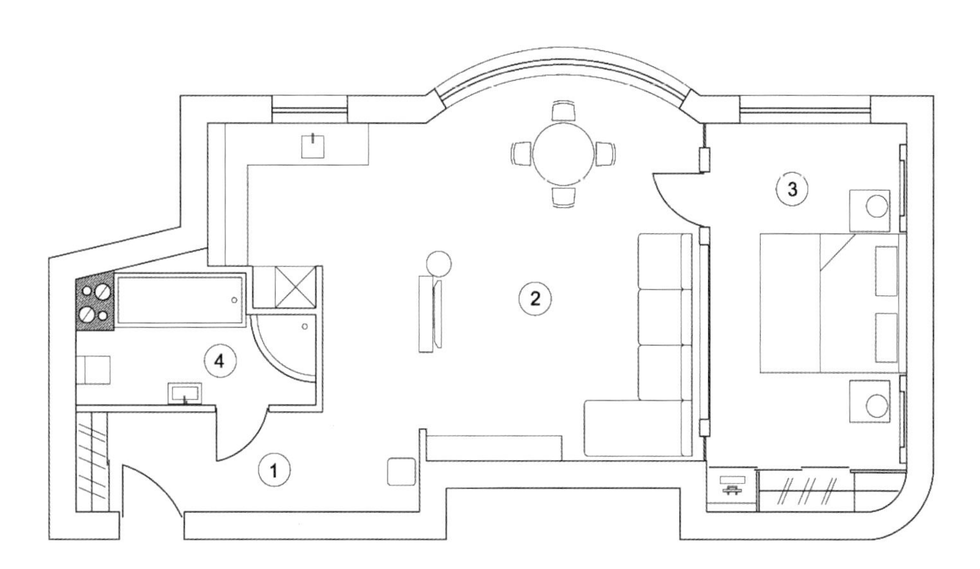

The interior includes vintage accessories, modern and Neo-baroque furniture, retro 1960s elements, a sculpture panel of an ancient arch, and high-tech materials and technology such as glass with diode illumination.

Apartment Adventurer

The apartment is located in a house on the border of an old town and sea port zone. The windows provide a view of port docks, dry-cargo ships on a quay and passengers arriving at the port. The client here has bright with unique personality, likes adventures and travelling, but still appreciates the comforts of home.

These factors made the designers of ERGES create an interior that reflected the personality of the owner, while maintaining the mysterious and intriguing environment of the location. The designers settled on making the space luxurious, free and eclectic and at the same time well-organised space. On planning the design, they decided to fill the whole interior with art objects and accessories and elegant and exotic decorations, together with renowned brand furniture and separate pieces produced by ERGES.

These include: a decorative glass column, a bar, mirrored furniture and an aquarium with reflective effects. In the interior, the designers put together the following materials: wood, glass, stainless steel, fur and natural stone. The design aimed to create a modern, comfortable and luxurious interior which corresponded to the flat's owner gentlemanly and adventurous disposition.

Name of Project:
An Apartment For A Gentleman (An Adventurer).
Location:
Riga, Latvia
Completion Date:
2007
Interior Design:
Erges architecture & design, Serge Serpuhov, Dmitry Yukhnevich
Photography:
Martin Kudrjavcev.
Client:
A gentleman

Highlight: The designers of ERGES created an interior that reflected the personality of the owner, while maintaining the mysterious and intriguing environment of the location.

The designers filled the whole interior with art objects and accessories and elegant and exotic decorations, together with renowned brand furniture and separate pieces produced by ERGES.

775 King Street West

Featuring dark colours that are dramatic yet appealing, the two beds plus den model suite are extremely characteristic in this project by II BY IV Design Associates. The 92 square metre suite features tones of blue and black accented with white and walnut colours.

The drama and balance of the dark on bright colours in the space y makes a case for home buyers to use any colour range inside a condominium home, as traditional people have steered away from darker colours with the misconception that it renders a space crammed. However, II BY IV has designed a perfect model suite. This particular floor plan features not only two bedrooms, but also a huge living space perfect for young professionals and singles who frequently entertain.

The suite layout also features a dining area fit for regular-sized dining tables and a large living room in with black finishes coupled with the distinct look of stainless steel appliances.

Name of Project:
775 King Street West
Location:
Toronto, Canada
Completion Date:
2010
Interior Design:
II BY IV Design Associates Inc.,
Dan Menchions,
Keith Rushbrook
Photography:
David Whittaker

Highlight: The suite balances dark on light colours with the drama and appeal.

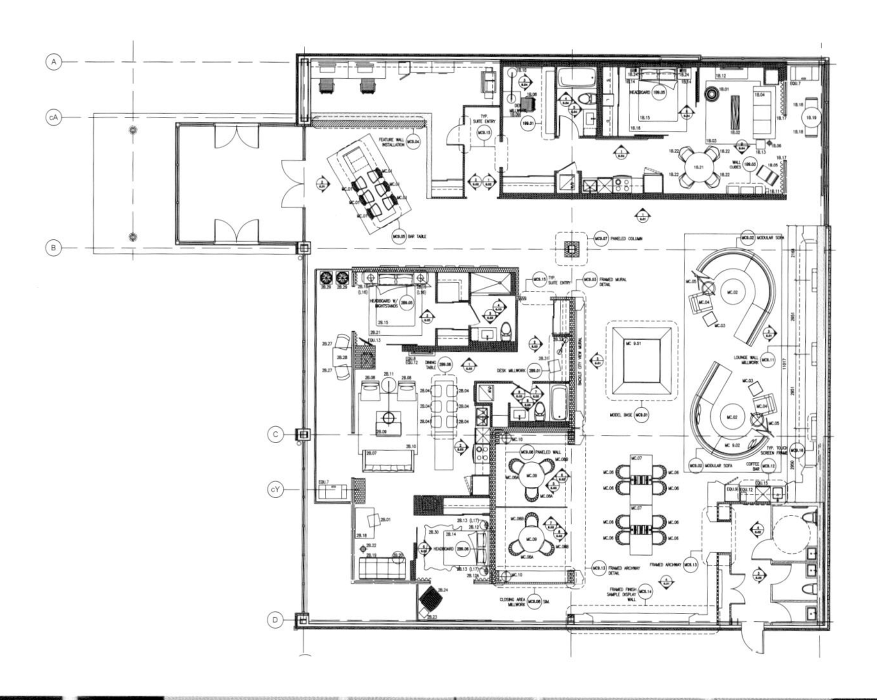

The suite features tones of blue and black accented with white and walnut colours, and floral wallpaper to create a warm bedroom atmosphere.

Mirror's House

How does architecture from the past adapt and respond to present and future requirements? A large house built during different periods in the 20th century has been adapted to current functional and aesthetic needs, without neglecting its historical and architectural value.

Original architectural elements of this house were restored and in some cases, reevaluated with a contemporary vision, which added contemporary design and new materials to the existing architecture. A mix of new and old was the goal of the interior design – contemporary furniture with clear and simple lines coexists with antique pieces that possess the ornamental value of their respective era.

Old concepts like wall stencils were a source of inspiration. Big free style patterns and bright colours stand out from the neutral white walls. The Mirror's House maintains this communication between the old and the new without a judging or subjugating either.

Name of Project:
Mirror's House
Location:
Merida, Mexico
Completion Date:
2007
Interior Design:
Estilo Arquitectura,
Víctor Alejandro Cruz Domínguez,
Iván Atahualpa Hernández Salazar,
Luis Estrada Aguilar
Photography:
Roberto Cardenas Cabello

Highlight: Mirror's House is a large old house has been adapted to current functional and esthetic needs.

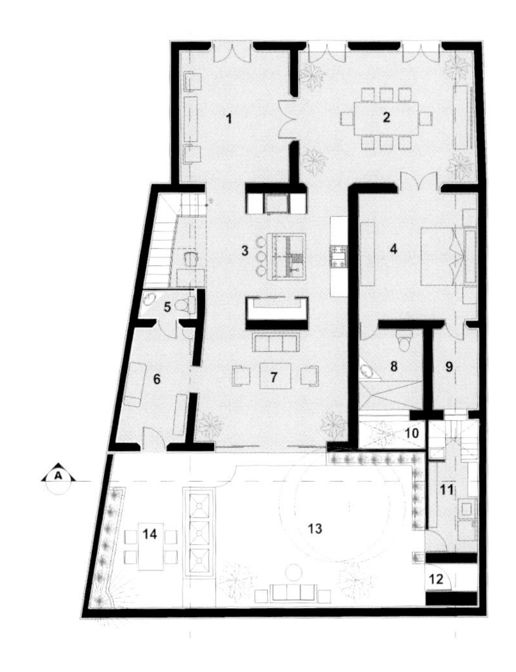
1
2
3
4
5
6
7
8
9
10
11
12
13
14
A

Big free style patterns and bright colours stand out
from the neutral white walls.

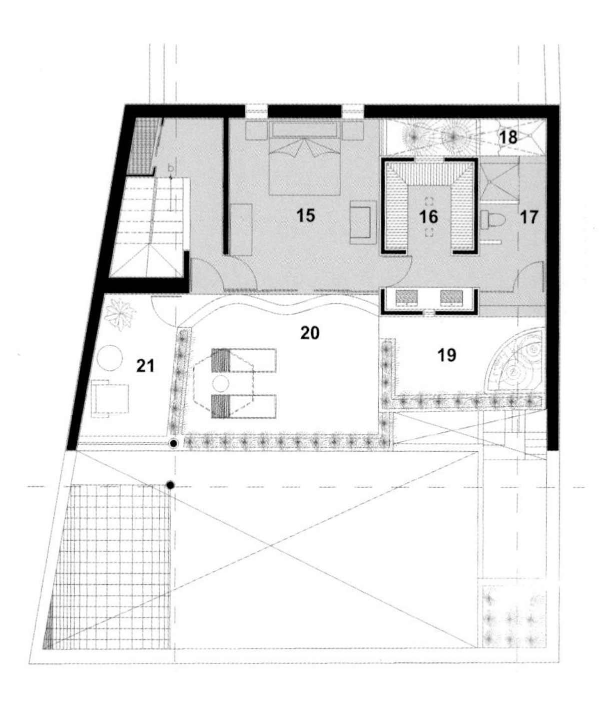

18
15
16
17
20
19
21

Atlantica Avenue

The apartment is located in a modern residential building that was built in the 1950s along the shore. It was designed for a single person who loves to entertain friends. The client looked for Arthur Casas because of the aesthetic affinities between the client and architect, which resulted in the concept being promptly approved.

The designers aimed to create wide rooms to enjoy the beautiful seascape, entertain friends and work in. This apartment is all about beige and neutral tones. Using beige and neutral colours, they highlight the architecture and the furniture design. The design of the working station with beige chairs and columns in the spacious room adds a unique effect.

The long bench beside the windows functions as a relaxation area, and other decorative elements including wall paintings, sculptures and books add artistic charm to the space.

Name of Project:
Atlantica Avenue apartment
Location:
Rio de Janeiro, Brazil
Completion Date:
2010
Interior Design:
Studio Arthur Casas Architecture and Design
Photography:
Tuca Reinés

Highlight: The designers aimed to create wide rooms to enjoy the beautiful seascape.

BEDROOM 03
BATHROOM 02
BEDROOM 02
MASTER BEDROOM
CLOSET
OFFICE
LIVING ROOM
CORRIDOR
MAIN ENTRY HALL
ELEVADOR SOCIAL
BED LINEN CLOTHES
BATHROOM 03
ELEVADOR SERVIÇO
SERVICE ENTRY
POWDER ROOM
STORAGE
DINING ROOM
SERVICE AREA
KITCHEN
PANTRY
SERVICE BEDROOM 1
SERVICE BEDROOM 2
GOURMET KITCHEN/ LIBRARY

667-999
33-4-666
001-333

A VIDA É BELA

GILBERT & GEORGE

The long bench beside the windows functions as a relaxation area, and other decorative elements including wall paintings, sculptures and books add artistic charm to the space.

FLUTUANDO NO ESPAÇO
UM SONHO
DAQUELES
QUE
PRECISAMOS
DE TODA
SUA FORÇA

A VIDA É BELA !!!

Rising Glen

Perched above Sunset Boulevard in Los Angeles, the renovation of this 1980s house called for a timeless, modern design.

The previously dark and confined residence was transformed into a clean and simple space. The newly designed kitchen opens up onto an exterior patio and fireplace where film and photographs can be projected onto a conserved wall. Large glass sliders link the kitchen environment to the exterior patios to the north and south, diminishing the difference between room and landscape.

Conceptually, the outdoor patio areas serve as extensions of the kitchen where people can use the interior and exterior space interchangeably.

Name of Project:
Rising Glen
Location:
Los Angeles, USA
Completion Date:
2007
Interior Design:
Montalba Architects, Inc.
Photography:
Dominique Vorillon

Highlight: The renovation of this 1980s house called for a timeless and modern design.

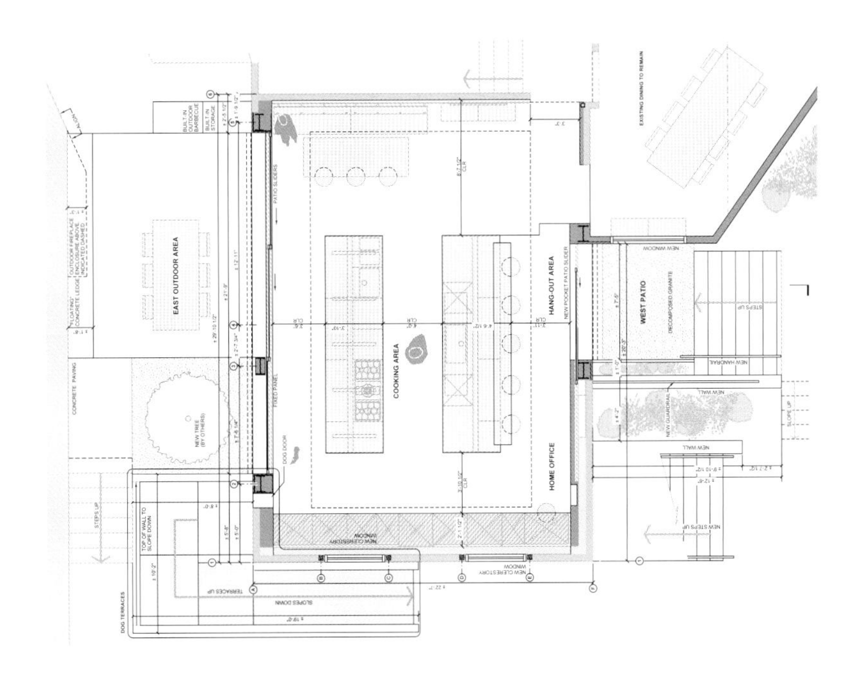
EAST OUTDOOR AREA
COOKING AREA
HANG-OUT AREA
HOME OFFICE
WEST PATIO

Pause

Slemdal Oslo

Returning from a two-year work engagement in New York, the owners wanted a continental apartment with a warm atmosphere as a backdrop for their own, colourful furnishings and art.

They decided on a grey and beige colour palette with focus on natural materials as wood and stones. Most of the permanent interior elements such as the kitchen counters, bathroom cabinets, the library, wardrobes, beds and tables were specially designed by Scenario for the project in collaboration with the owner himself and Terna Snekkeri. Scenario was also responsible for designing the fireplace and the indoor stairs. There was a great emphasis on lighting in the project, especially with regard to the presentation of the owner's art and antiques.

On the main floor, living room, kitchen, library and master bedroom, all lighting was delivered by XAL, a Switzerland-based company. Integrated and indirect lighting was combined with wall washers and spotlights, making the whole space exude a harmonious, circuitous and unique flavour.

Name of Project:
House Slemdal Oslo
Location:
Oslo, Norway
Completion Date:
2008
Interior Design:
AS Scenario Interiørarkiteter MNIL
Photography:
Sveinung Bråthen and Scenario Interiørarkitekter

Highlight: House Slemdal Oslo is a continental apartment with a warm atmosphere as a backdrop for colourful furnishings and art.

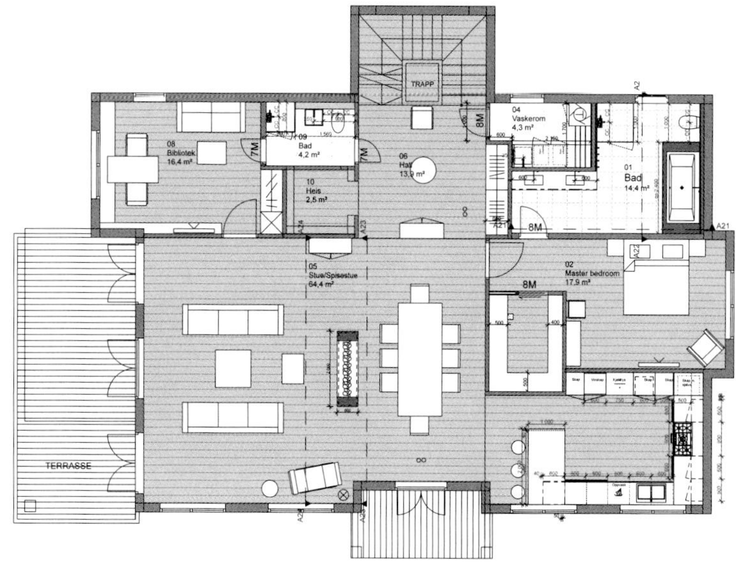
TRAPP
04
Vaskerom
4,3 m²
08
Bibliotek
16,4 m²
09
Bad
4,2 m²
06
Hall
13,9 m²
01
Bad
14,4 m²
10
Heis
2,5 m²
05
Stue/Spisestue
64,4 m²
02
Master bedroom
17,9 m²
TERRASSE

15 Broad Street

Axis Mundi completed two residences for a brother and a sister at Downtown by Starck at 15 Broad Street. The brother owns an extensive collection of art works by the Japanese artist Takashi Murakami which is displayed in a salon style and is the main focus of the space.

Other highlights include a six metre long red silk velvet-covered banquette, lighting fixtures by Droog, table lamps by Starck, and furniture by Moooi. Red is the predominant colour throughout. The sister's apartment is somewhat smaller and more subdued. The main design element is a glass room with sliding panels which serves as her bedroom.

Golden silk drapes line the interior to make the space more soft and elegant. Most of the furniture, built-ins and silk carpets were custom designed specifically as space was at a premium. All of the rooms serve multiple functions.

Name of Project:
15 Broad Street
Location:
New York , USA
Completion Date:
2008
Interior Design:
Axis Mundi,
John Beckmann,
Richard Rosenbloom
Photography:
Mikiko Kikuyama
Client:
Anonymous

Highlight: All of the rooms serve multiple functions.

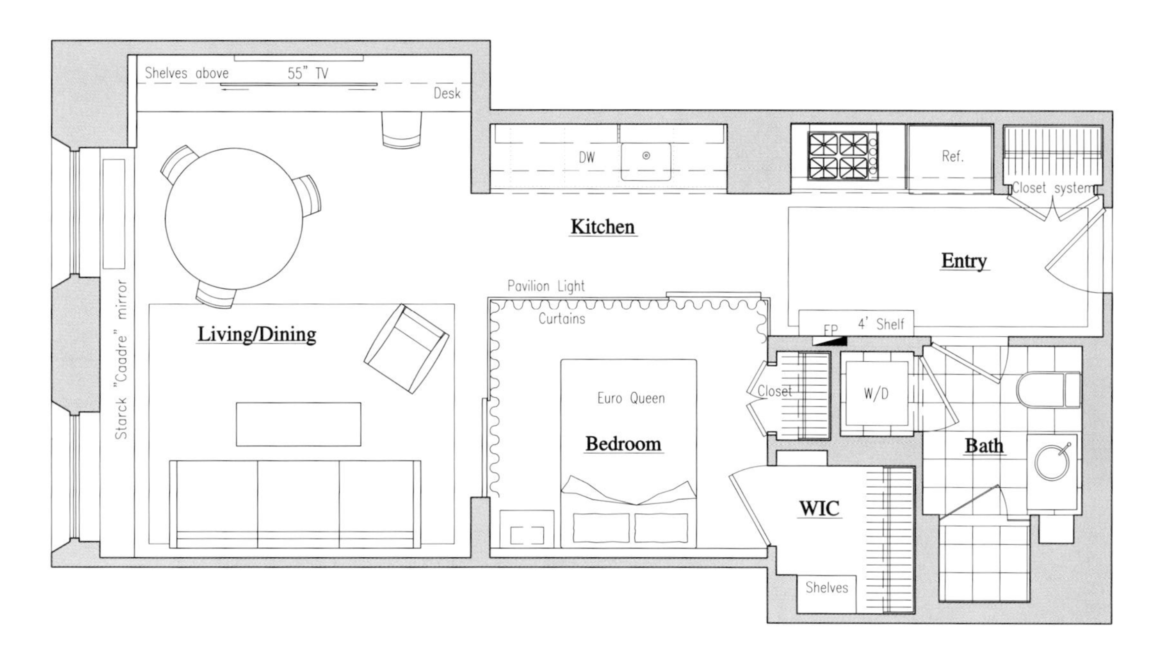
Shelves above
55" TV
Desk
DW
Ref.
Closet system
Kitchen
Entry
Pavilion Light
Curtains
Living/Dining
Starck "Caadre" mirror
FP
4' Shelf
Euro Queen
Bedroom
Closet
W/D
Bath
WIC
Shelves

The main design element is a glass room with sliding panels which serves as her bedroom. Golden silk drapes line the interior to make the space more soft and elegant.

NEW YORK 1960

NEW YORK 1960

Artworks are displayed in a salon style while a custom silk shag carpet, based on animal patterns, was designed for the living area.

A GRAND ITALIAN EPIC

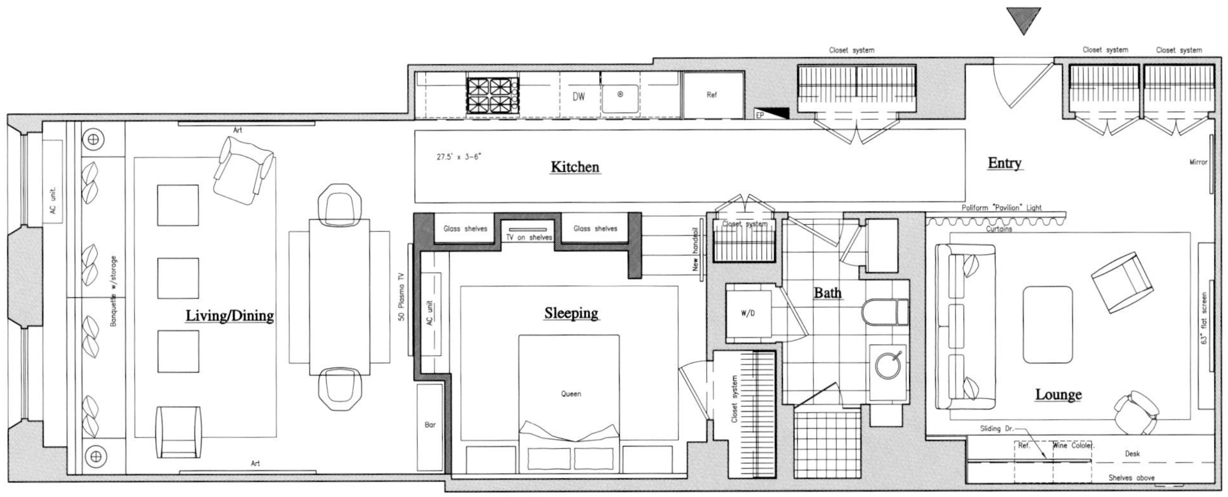
Closet system
Closet system
Closet system
DW
Ref
EP
Art
AC unit.
27.5' x 3-6"
Kitchen
Entry
Mirror
Glass shelves
TV on shelves
Glass shelves
New handrail
Closet system
Poliform "Pavilion" Light
Curtains
Banquette w/storage
Living/Dining
50 Plasma TV
AC unit
Sleeping
Bath
W/D
63" flat screen
Queen
Closet system
Lounge
Bar
Sliding Dr.
Ref.
Wine Cololer.
Desk
Shelves above
Art

Forbes Townhouse

This project upgrades Brooklyn brownstone in the Park Slope Historic District in a distinctive manner. The clients are both trained in the visual arts, and have well-developed sensibilities about how a house is used, as well as how elements from certain eras can interact visually. A lively dialogue has resulted in a design in which the architectural and construction interventions serve as a subtle background to the decorating.

The intended effect was for each room to have a timeless quality, while the fit-ups, loose furniture, and lighting appear more contemporary. Thus, the bathrooms are sheathed in mosaic tile with a rough texture and the overall colour palette is generally muted. The family kitchen features rough brick walls and exposed wood beams while the kitchen cabinets are modern, overlaid with slabs of walnut veneer.

Throughout the house, visible components include thick Cararra marble, mahogany windows with weights-and-pulleys, steel sash windows and doors, and period light fixtures. What is not seen is a state-of-the-art infrastructure consisting of a new hot water plant, structured cabling, new electrical connections and plumbing.

Name of Project:
Forbes Townhouse
Location:
Brooklyn, USA
Completion Date:
2007
Interior Design:
Abelow Sherman Architects
Photography:
Mikiko Kikuyama
Client:
Adam and Amy Forbes

Highlight: Forbes Townhouse's design is one in which the architectural and construction interventions serve as a subtle background to the decorating.

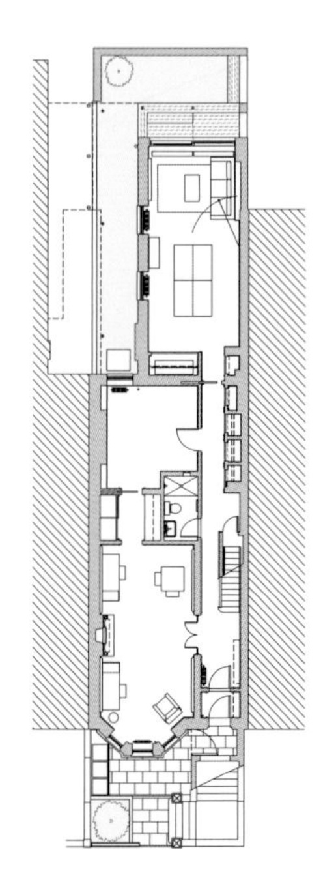

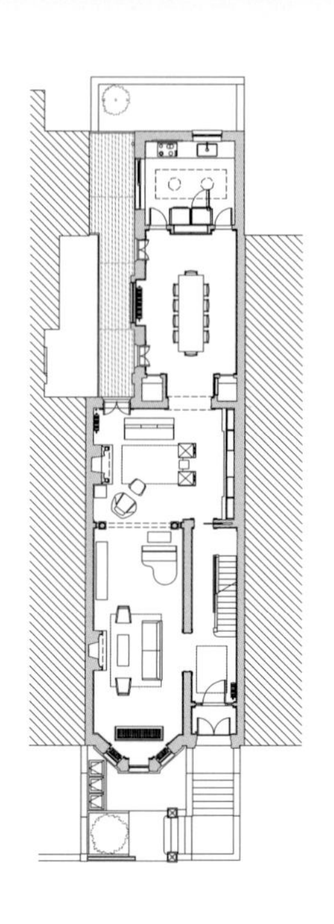

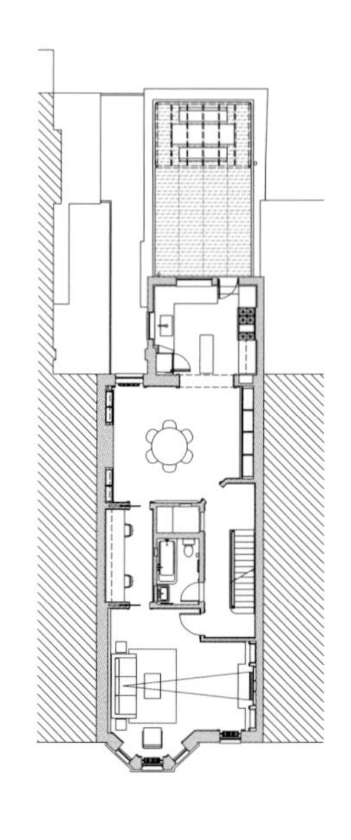

Throughout the house, visible components include thick Cararra marble, mahogany windows with weights-and-pulleys, steel sash windows and doors, and period light fixtures.

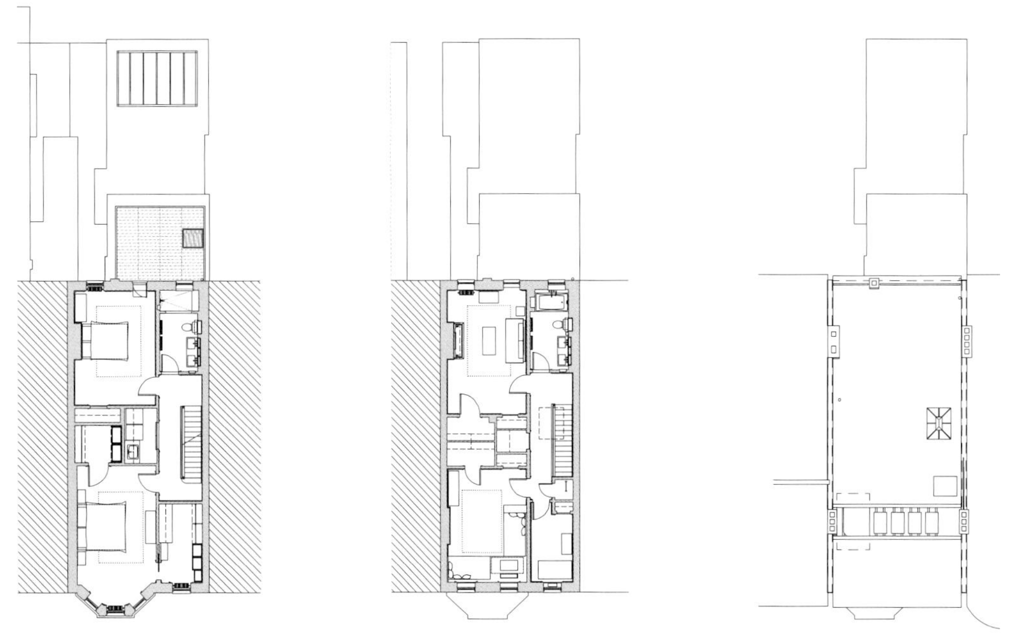

Cass Gilbert Residence

This 360 square metre residence has a 360 degree view of the entire city, with full terraces running along both the north and south sides of the building.

The owner was looking for a home to house his extensive 1940's Italian furniture and contemporary art collection. The living room has three horizons: in the north and south, full walls of steel-framed glass windows frame the panoramic view, while on the eastern wall, a six metre Wim Wenders C-print, Dust Road West Australia 1988, creates the third unexpected horizon.

The restored Assyrian-styled facade stands in stark contrast to the free flowing 1993 Julian Schnabel oil collage/painting. A rare 1940's Italian carved ash desk by Aldo Maria Scorcia shares the study with a varied collection of deities housed in the lacquered niches of the walnut "wall of gods".

Name of Project:
Cass Gilbert Residence
Locati on:
New York, USA
Completion Date:
2007
Interior Design:
Koko Architecture + Design,
Adam Weintraub;
Mishi Hosono;
Eiko Sakai
Photography:
Mikiko Kikuyama
Client:
Cass Gilbert

Highlight: This 360 square metre residence has a 360 degree view of the entire city.

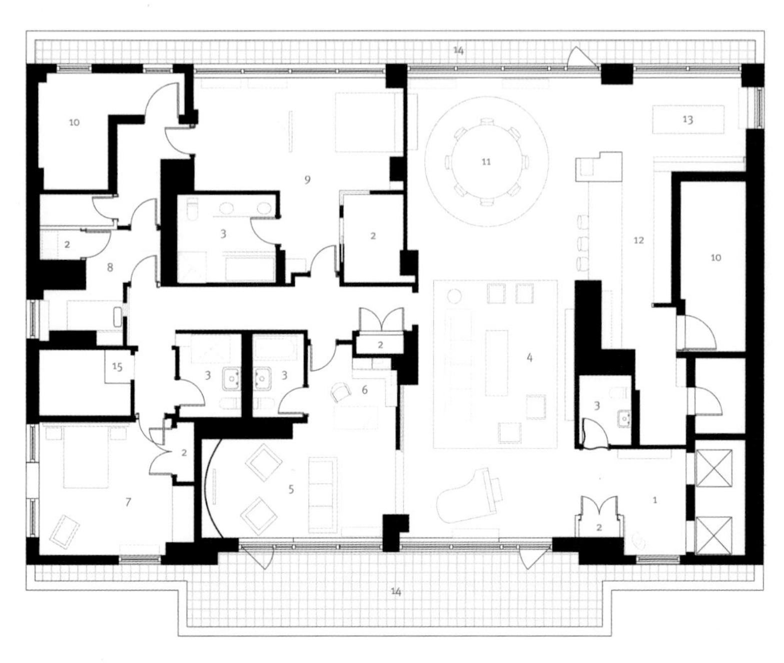
14
10
9
11
13
3
2
12
10
2
8
15
3
3
6
4
2
3
2
7
5
1
2
14

The strong afternoon light bounces off the vintage Fontana Arte chandelier and passes over the 3 metre in diameter walnut dining table, finally resting on the custom round Emma Gardner silk rug.

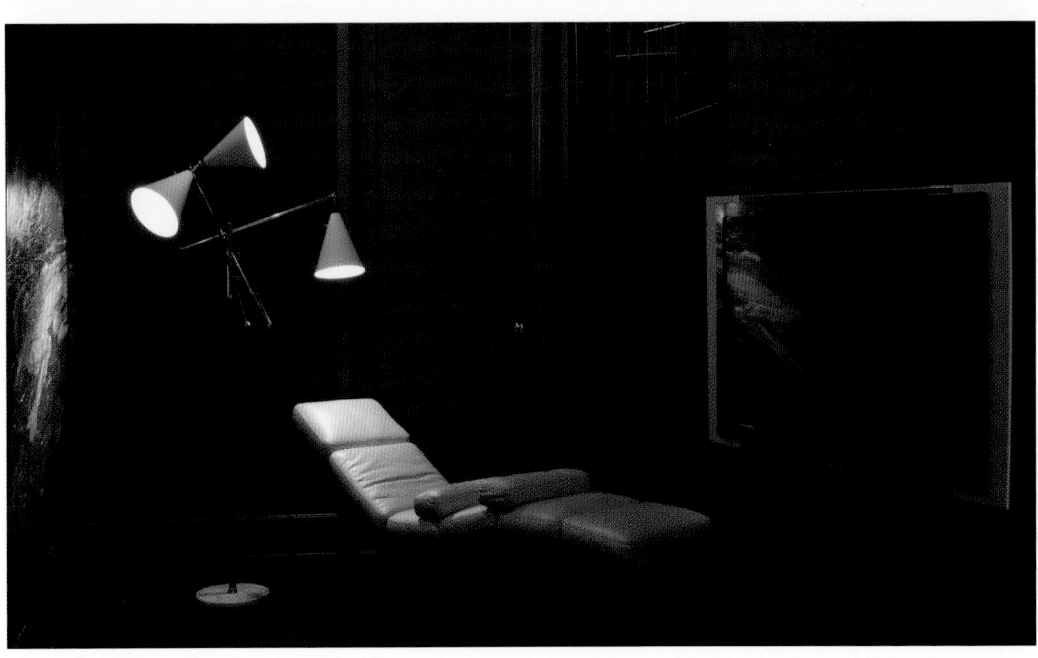

Moss House

The beautiful Moss House is a private residence in the Ebisu area of Tokyo, Japan. The house accumulates some strange and wonderful features – an oddly long hallway and a tiny room–from a series of earlier renovations, so the designers decided to build on these earlier features, and to acclimatise the space to the new owner's lifestyle.

Most wallpaper imitates nature through a two-dimensional representation of it, and cladding the walls entirely in moss would be too much. They wanted something in-between, so they applied the dried moss in a vine-like pattern that looked like wallpaper, creating an ambiguous texture that's neither artificial nor natural.

In additions, the same pattern appears on the cable outlet, doorframes and door handles, further synthesizing the moss pattern with the space. The result imparts a striking, textural quality, a perfect twist on traditional wallpaper patterns.

Name of Project:
Moss House
Location:
Tokyo, Japan
Completion Date:
2008
Interior Design:
Nendo,
Oki Sato
Photography:
Daici Ano

Highlight: The dried moss creates an ambiguous texture that is neither artificial nor natural.

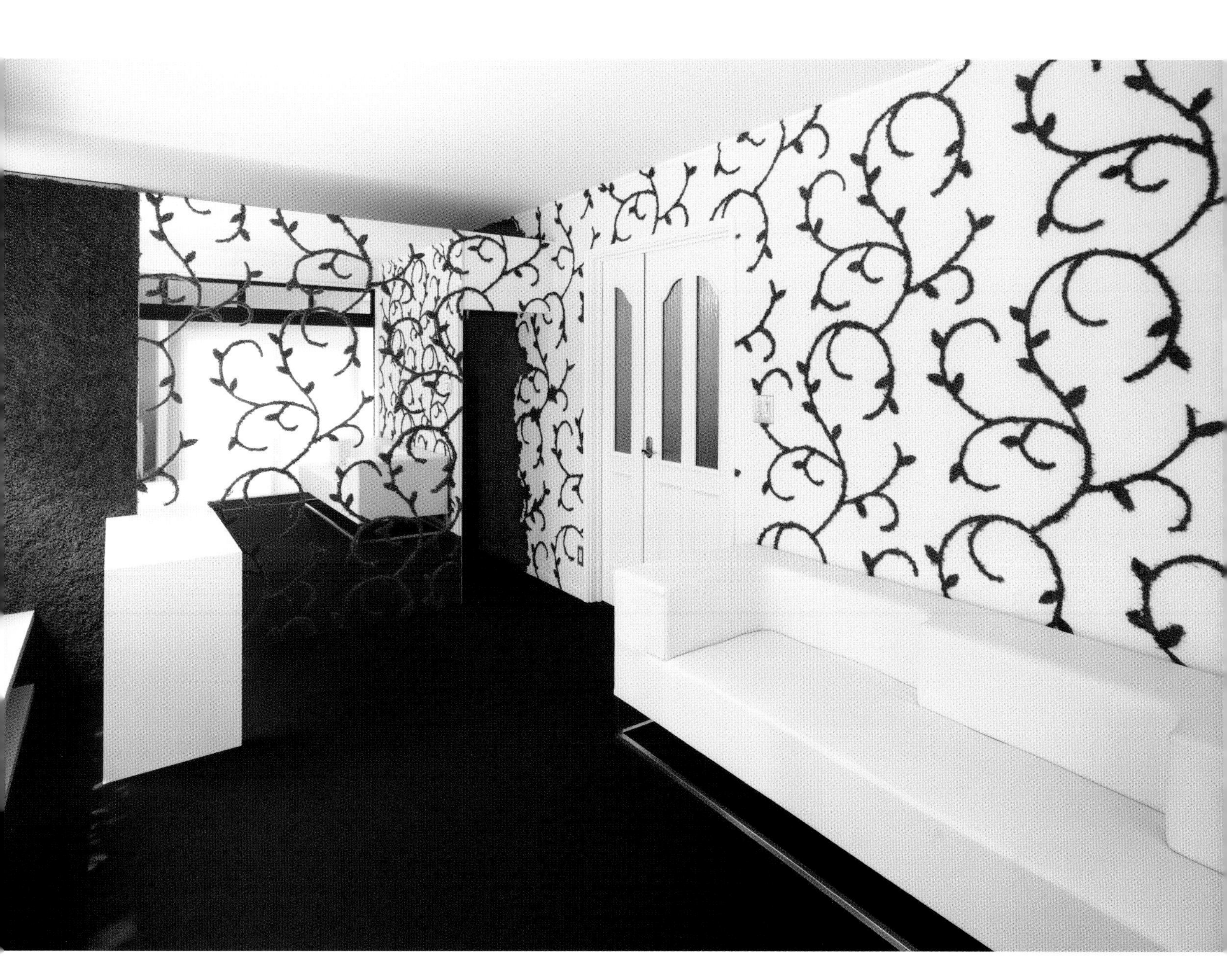

Designers applied the dry moss in a vine-like pattern that looks like wallpaper on the interior walls to subtly connect the house's interior environment with its exterior one.

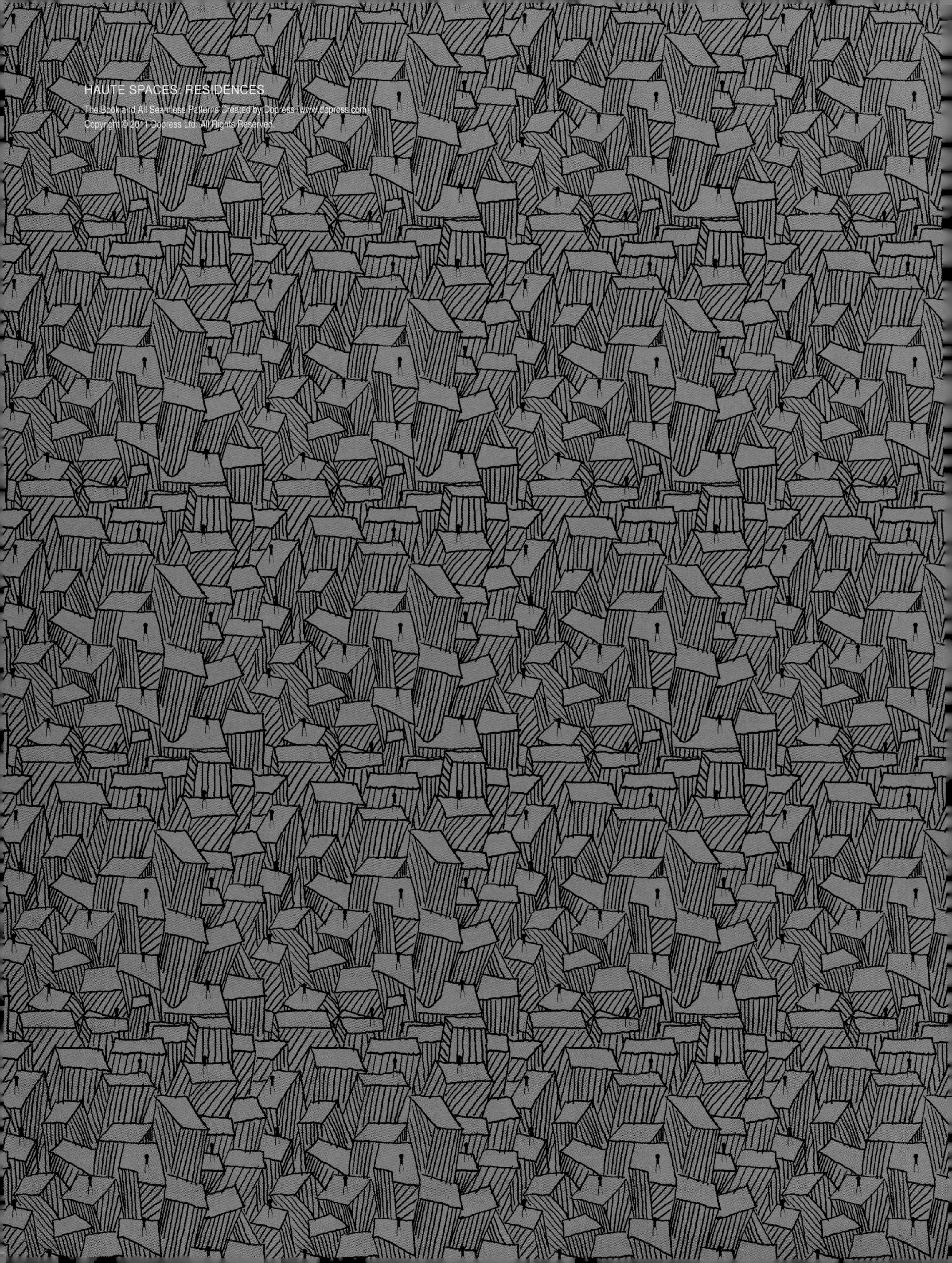
HAUTE SPACES: RESIDENCES
The Book and All Seamless Patterns Created by Dopress (www.dopress.com).
Copyright © 2011 Dopress Ltd. All Rights Reserved.

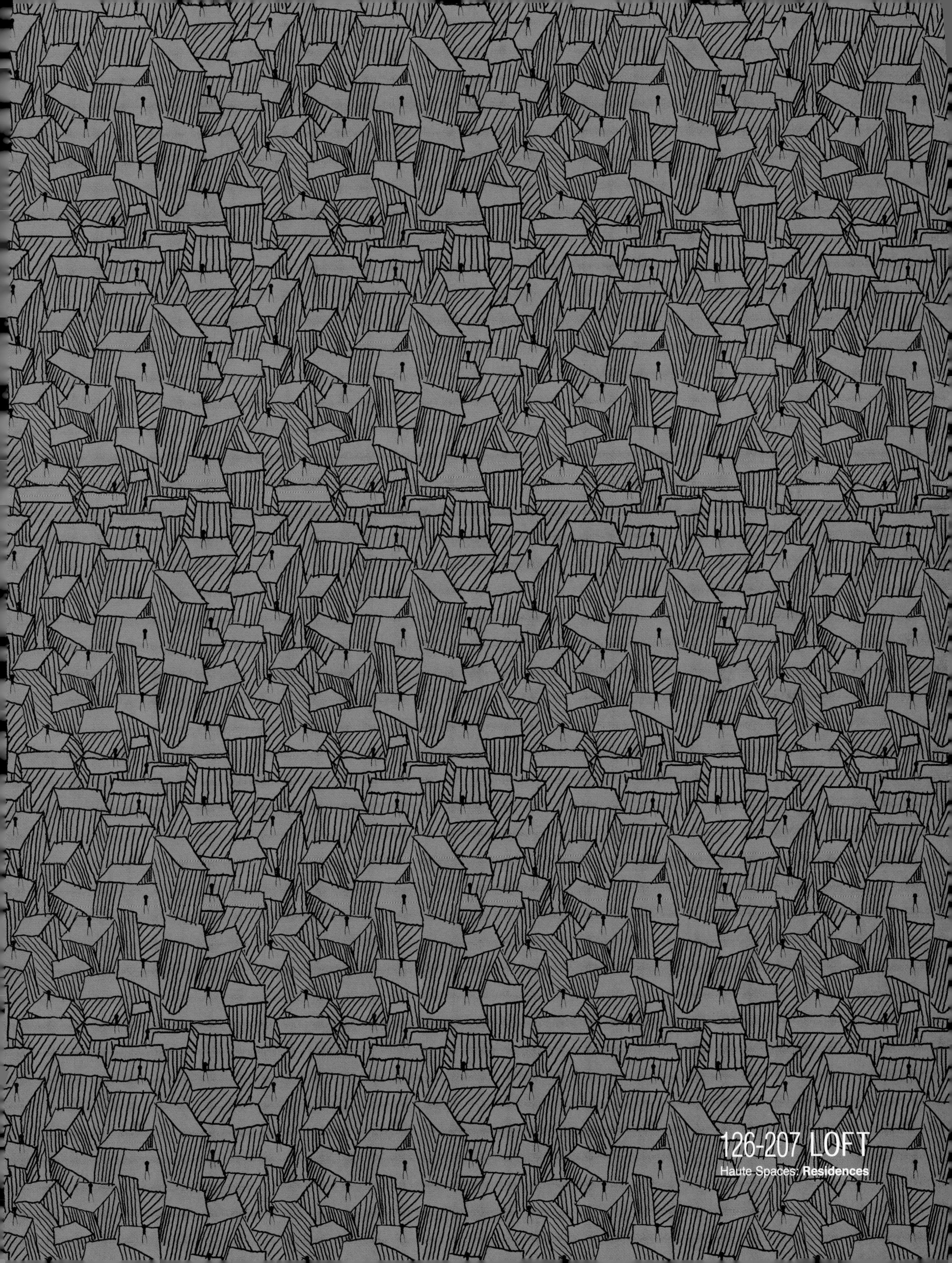
126-207 LOFT
Haute Spaces: **Residences**

Kenig Residence

The program of spaces was organized by floor. The basement was finished to become a casual family dentype room with a pool table and couches, etc. The ground floor level was opened up to become a loft-like living room and kitchen with an exterior wood deck floating outside, over the backyard. The second floor became the girls' floor with bedrooms, a study, kid-lounge and bath. Bachelor retreat was the idea of the third and top floor, with a home office, bedroom and bath.

Tying the home together, the stair acts as a spine from basement to the third floor. A new skylight was inserted into the roof, above the stair, accentuating the vertical rise and bringing natural light down into the home. The wall behind the stair was finished with sheets of blackened steel that run continuously from the parlour level to the roof. Display elements can be easily affixed to the wall using magnets.

By creating an entirely flexible canvas of metal, the designers offered a space with infinite possibilities for visuals. The flexibility of the magnet wall fosters the organic creation of zones, as people affix items of interest to them at their own floor – alternatively, the entire stair could be rigorously curated.

Name of Project:
Kenig Residence
Location:
Brooklyn, USA
Completion Date:
2007
Interior Design:
Slade Architecture
Photography:
Jordi Miralles
Client:
Ricky Kenig

Highlight: The ground floor level was opened up to become a loft-like living room.

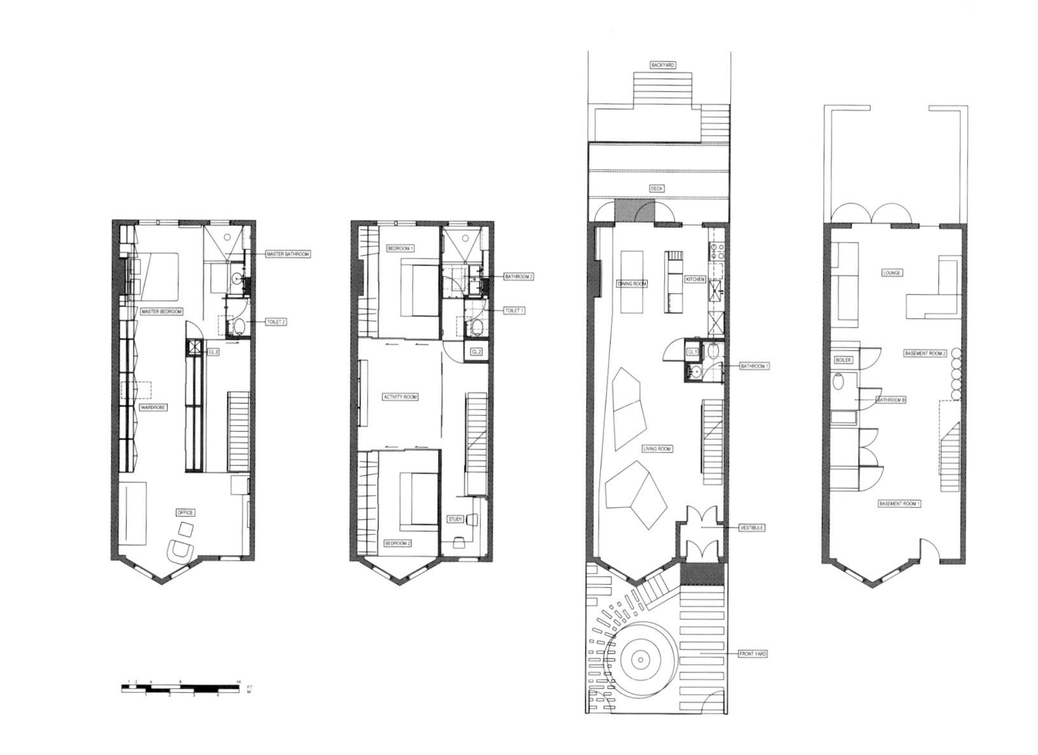
BACKYARD
MASTER BATHROOM
MASTER BEDROOM
TOILET 2
CL.3
WARDROBE
OFFICE
BEDROOM 1
BATHROOM 2
TOILET 1
CL.2
ACTIVITY ROOM
STUDY
BEDROOM 2
DECK
DINING ROOM
KITCHEN
CL.1
BATHROOM 1
LIVING ROOM
VESTIBULE
FRONT YARD
LOUNGE
BOILER
BASEMENT ROOM 2
BATHROOM B
BASEMENT ROOM 1

The wall behind the stair was finished with sheets of blackened steel that ran continuously from the parlor level to the roof. Display elements can be easily affixed to the wall using magnets.

Design
FLUX
All-American Ads
T-SHIRT
ERIC STANTON
ANIMAL PORTRAITS
NEW YORK
FASHION
WARHOL
marc newson
Dressing in the Dark
Philip Johnson

Artist's Loft Apartment

The project was designed by CL3 Architects Ltd. Artist's Loft Apartment combines sleeping, working and entertaining, and aims to achieve sustainable design by using recycled materials and furniture.

Situated in the south of Hong Kong Island, the design maximises the exposure to daylight and the ocean view. The raw finish exterior walls and fair face brick partitions add natural texture to the space and also reduce usage of construction materials and wastage.

The furniture selection mixes new and reused furniture, blending Chinese antique and contemporary furniture. The plastic laminate dining table is also used as the artist's work station. A step ladder leads to the sleeping area above the toilet and pantry area.

Name of Project:
Artist's Loft Apartment
Location:
Hong Kong, China
Completion Date:
2009
Interior Design:
CL3 Architects Ltd,
William Lim
Photography:
Nirut Benjabanpot

Highlight: Artist's Loft Apartment aims to achieve sustainable design by using recycled materials and furniture.

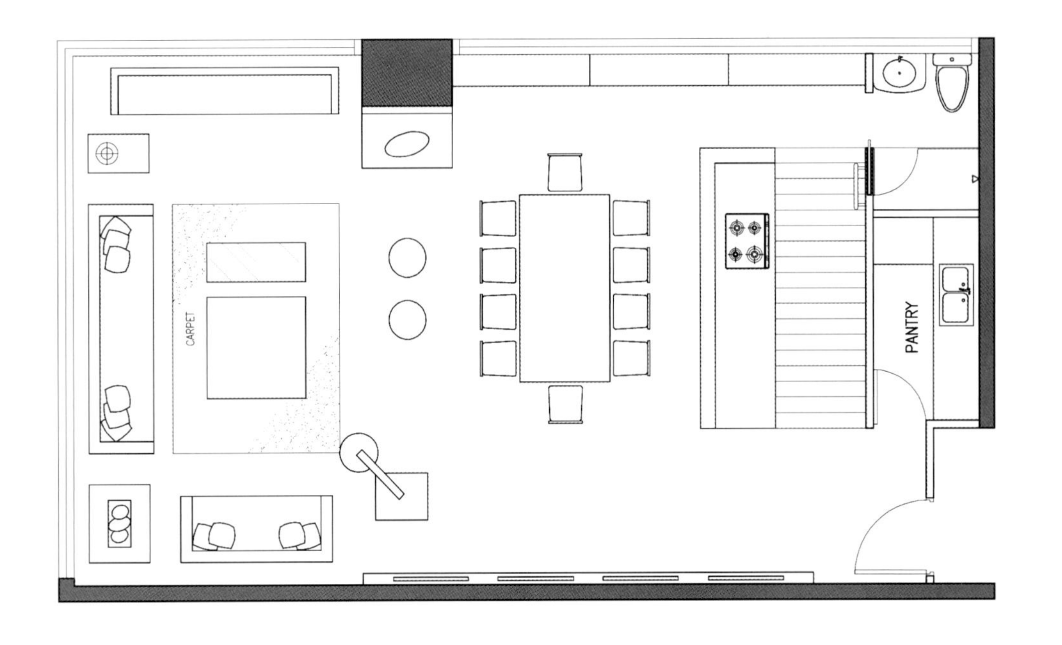
CARPET
PANTRY

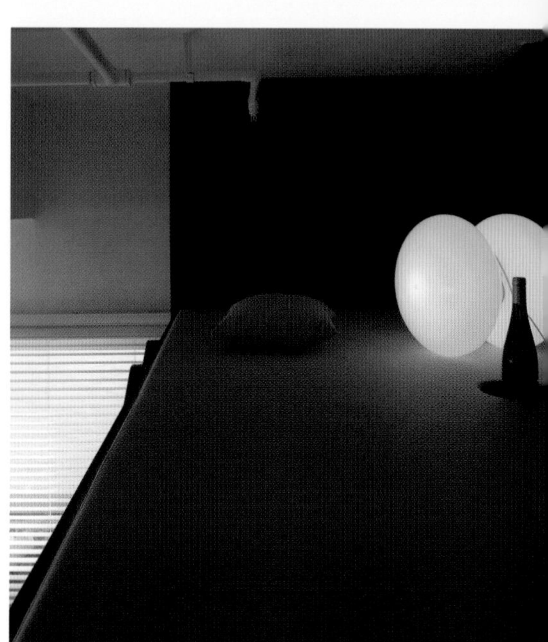

The raw finish exterior walls and fair face brick partitions add natural texture to the space. The furniture selection mixes new and reused furniture, blending Chinese antique and contemporary furniture.

Art|Basel|Miami Beach
4–7|Dec|2008

Micheli House

The genesis of the plan of the House in Florence by Simone Micheli where he lives together with his wife Roberta and his son Cesar, lies its foundations in the concept of modern luxury the Tuscan architect developed.

Simone Micheli asserted that "luxury does not mean immobility or habit, but rather freedom and movement. It is a light and stirring thought, at any moment we are able to choose where and how to live and to reinvent the environment we live in. As for architecture the new luxury is related to the idea of regaining the beauties and the truth of our daily life together with our inner feelings. It is more connected with vacuums than with plenums, more with mind than with body.

It does not mean opulence but rather transparency. I am talking about possible places where yours and their histories are echoing in the shape of visual, olfactory, tactile and auditory essence."

Name of Project:
Micheli House
Location:
Florence, Italy
Completion Date:
2009
Interior Design:
Simone Micheli
Photography:
Juergen Eheim
Client:
Simone Micheli

Highlight: Luxury does not mean immobility or habit, but rather freedom and movement.

to
dream
or...

In this project, the designer was telling you a story which has its roots in the past and in the tastes of exotic places but at the same time it is near and next future oriented.

10×10

Amsterdam Loft

UXUS are pleased to present a private residence located in a historic building along one of Amsterdam's famous canals. The home is located in a 250 square metre 18th century warehouse with a panoramic view over the city.

The interior of the loft situated in an old sugar warehouse built in 1763, had remained in its original state for almost 250 years and the owners wanted to keep as much intact with as little intervention to the space as possible. In keeping the original open-plan layout, UXUS created a series of dramatic curtain walls that could be opened and closed according to the needs of use. Made of luxurious Italian linen, the curtain walls are opaque when lit from the front yet transparent from behind.

At night, the space becomes a series of glowing tents, creating the effect of a surreal interior landscape. All of the decorative interior elements were selected to reflect the eclectic tastes of the owners.

Name of Project:
Amsterdam Loft
Location:
Amsterdam, Netherlands
Completion Date:
2003
Interior Design:
UXUS
Photography:
Dim Balsem

Highlight: The Amsterdam Loft is a private residence located in a historic building along one of Amsterdam's famous canals.

In keeping the original open-plan layout, a series of dramatic curtain walls were created. Made of luxurious Italian linen, the curtain walls could be opened and closed according to the needs of use.

Ensanche Flat

The alteration of the flat is a re-reading of the spatial structure of the typical Barcelona Ensanche flat at the end of the 19th century – a succession of isolated rooms and disconnected courts. The designers dissolved the structure of walls through physical and visual connections.

The restructuring of the former flat gives the space an unexpected effect whose origin remains in the principal room. In the living space, the golden lines establish a horizontal division in the flat: up to 2.2 metres between each portion with the one above holding mezzanines of storage, bottle racks and an entry of zenithal light in the bath or the polyvalent room.

The flat is a fresh dialogue between the golden ceiling art in the dining room and the illuminated drops of water. The stairs are decorated by mosaic patterns in retro style, which resembles a collage of magical carpet.

Name of Project:
Ensanche Flat
Location:
Barcelona, Spain.
Completion Date:
2007
Interior Design:
MIEL Architects
Photography:
Nelson Non,
Fran Parente
Client:
Nelson Non

Highlight: The alteration of the flat is a re-reading of the spatial structure of the typical Barcelona Ensanche flat at the end of the 19th century.

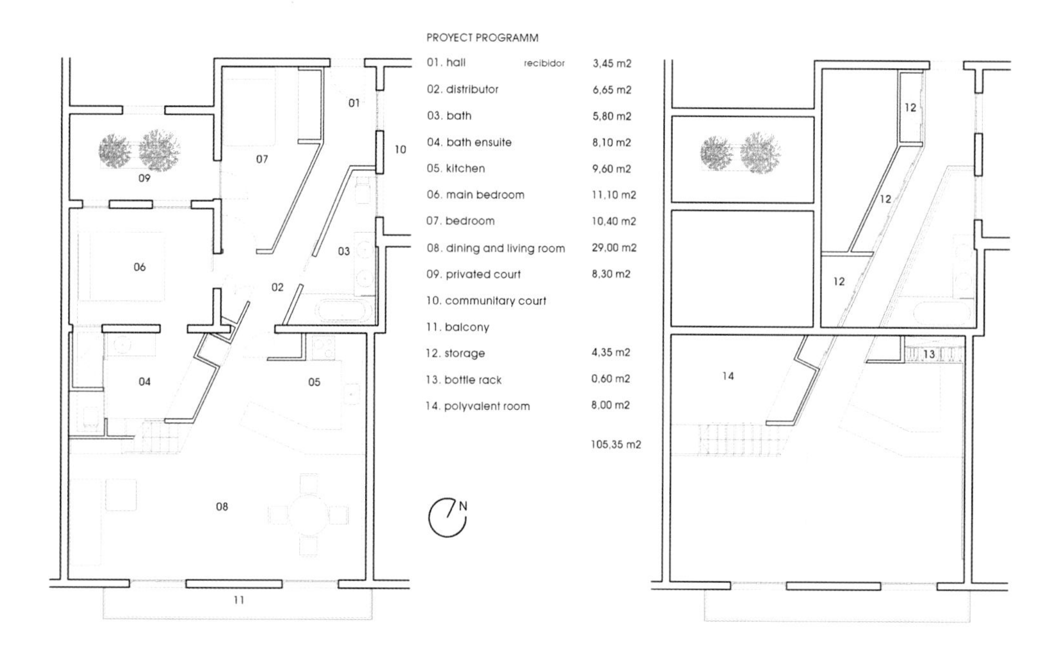
PROYECT PROGRAMM
01. hall recibidor 3,45 m2
02. distributor 6,65 m2
03. bath 5,80 m2
04. bath ensuite 8,10 m2
05. kitchen 9,60 m2
06. main bedroom 11,10 m2
07. bedroom 10,40 m2
08. dining and living room 29,00 m2
09. privated court 8,30 m2
10. communitary court
11. balcony
12. storage 4,35 m2
13. bottle rack 0,60 m2
14. polyvalent room 8,00 m2
105,35 m2
N

The flat is a fresh dialogue between the golden ceiling art in the dining room and the illuminated drops of water. The stairs are decorated by mosaic patterns in retro style, which resembles a collage of magical carpet.

LA Loft Los Angeles

The dwelling is located in an existing warehouse building in downtown Los Angeles. The living-working environment was designed for creative professionals. Two distinct entities are evident in the design. The angular geometry of the faceted stone-clad monolith stands in contrast to the free-flowing organic elliptical shaped room. Through these two pieces a dialogue begins to emerge.

Harmony and conflict co-exist within the dichotomous dwelling. Technology is used to control the environment as well as to design and fabricate the space. The building materials used were chosen for their ability to absorb or reflect the ever-changing colour palette of the light. The raised flooring transforms into the lounge seating area and the desk of the work station.

A spa area is provided with a stylised garden and floating steel fireplace. Undulating curved walls from the womb-like enclosure serves as the kitchen. The skin of the elliptical shaped room tears away, revealing the concealed bathroom.

Name of Project:
LA Loft
Location:
Los Angeles, USA
Completion Date:
2008
Interior Design:
Patrick Tighe Architecture.com
Photography:
Art Gray Photographer
Client:
Jef Sampson

Highlight: The living-working environment was designed for creative professionals.

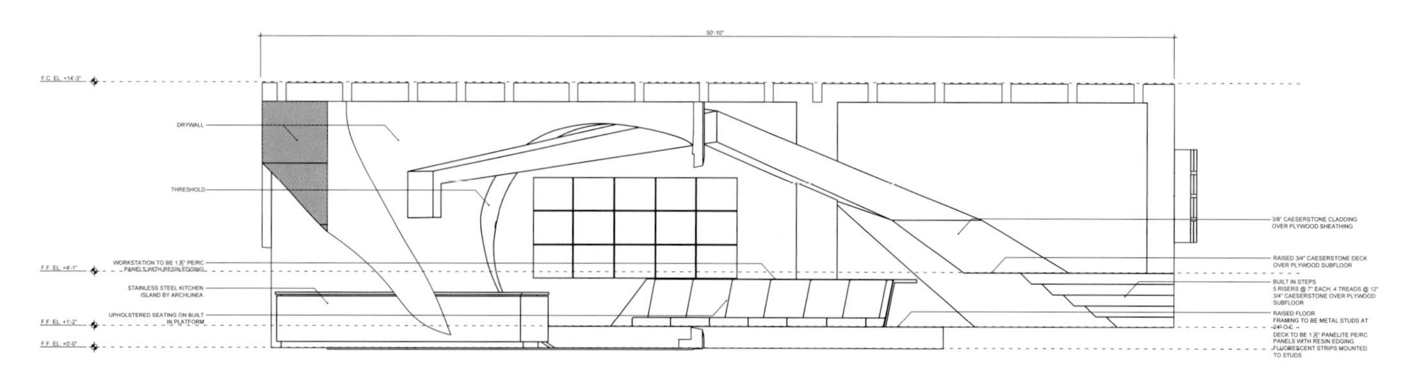
57'-10"
F.C. EL. +14'-3"
DRYWALL
THRESHOLD
WORKSTATION TO BE 1 ½" PE/RC PANELS WITH RESIN EDGING
F.F. EL. +4'-1"
STAINLESS STEEL KITCHEN ISLAND BY ARCHLINEA
UPHOLSTERED SEATING ON BUILT IN PLATFORM
F.F. EL. +1'-2"
F.F. EL. +0'-0"
3/8" CAESERSTONE CLADDING OVER PLYWOOD SHEATHING
RAISED 3/4" CAESERSTONE DECK OVER PLYWOOD SUBFLOOR
BUILT IN STEPS
5 RISERS @ 7" EACH, 4 TREADS @ 12"
3/4" CAESERSTONE OVER PLYWOOD SUBFLOOR
RAISED FLOOR
FRAMING TO BE METAL STUDS AT 24" O.C.
DECK TO BE 1 ½" PANELITE PE/RC PANELS WITH RESIN EDGING
FLUORESCENT STRIPS MOUNTED TO STUDS

The overhead cantilevered stone appendage penetrates the elliptical 'embryonic form'. The two distinct entities compliment, contrast, and violate one another as they coalesce into one.

Greenne Street Loft

The existing space is a commercial and industrial loft of about 300 square metres. The historic front and back industrial windows define the large loft feel. In order to emphasise these and to allow light and views into the 30 metre deep building, the designers kept the space very open from front to back.

Three 3 metre tall freestanding volumes arranged down the centre of the existing space define the different programme areas. The first volume is an aluminum bookcase which separates the living, dining and kitchen areas from the study. The side of the bookcase facing the living room is deep and is designed specifically to house the owner's collection of traditional Korean trunks. The side facing the study is more dense and shallow for shelving books.

The second volume contains a built-in desk area facing the study and a closet on the other side. Two hidden doors allow for a corridor between this volume and the third (the walk-in closet) to be closed off. The third volume contains the other side of the large walk-in closet and the master bathroom.

Name of Project:
Greenne Street Loft
Location:
New York, USA
Completion Date:
2007
Interior Design:
Slade Architecture
Photography:
Jordi Miralles

Highlight: The historic front and back industrial windows define the large loft feel.

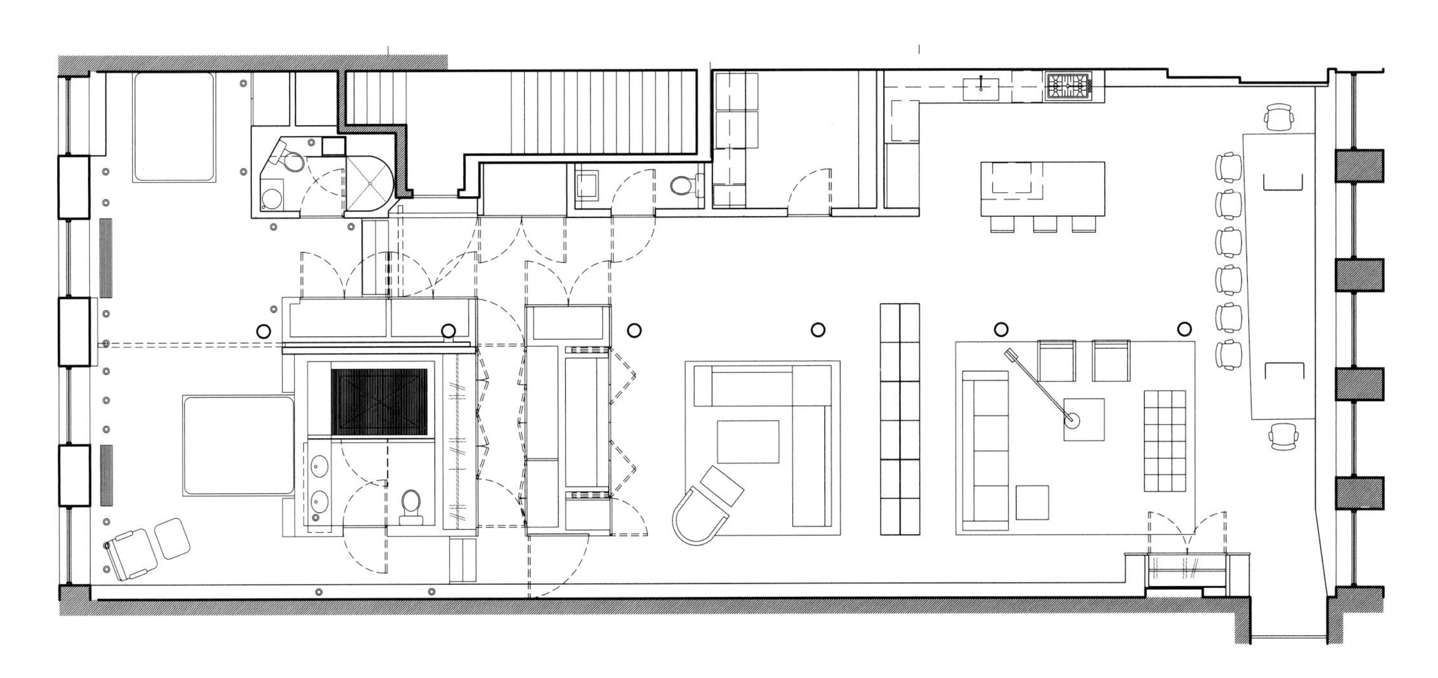

The aluminum bookcase separates the living, dining and kitchen areas from the study. The side of the bookcase facing the living room is deep and is designed specifically to house the owner's collection of traditional Korean trunks.

Three 3 metre tall freestanding volumes arranged down the centre of the existing space define the different programme areas.

Shuwai Residence

The project is located on the 7th and 8th floor of a 20-storey building in Pudong. There is a high-ceiling balcony connecting both floors' structures. At the entrance located on the lower floor, designers placed the staircase at the bottom, resembling the swivel hinge of the entire space.

On the one hand, it is used as a viewing deck of the entrance while on the other hand; it also divides and defines the entire space into left and right, up and down. They utilise the mirror on the ceiling to enlarge the left and right hidden vertical modelling cabinet in order to connect to and enlarge the focus point of the coloured glaze drop light to the upper and the lower floors. On the left of the staircase is the living room. The balcony of the living room has a high ceiling directly connected to the master bedroom. At the bottom of the balcony, designers place a two-storey-high mirror to magnify the entire space. To the right of the staircase is the dining room, which connects the Western and Chinese kitchen.

The ceiling has been cut hollow by approximately 60 centimetres to off set partial vision linking it to the study room. Following the staircase is to the private area on the second floor. Besides the master bedroom and secondary bedroom, all other spaces utilise a mobile separator as a way to bring together all sections of the home.

Name Of Project:
Shuwai Residence
Location:
Shanghai, China
Completion Date:
2009
Interior Design:
Mohen Design International,
Zhao Lu,
Wang Yongjian,
Hou Xianyong,
Luo Yulong
Photography:
Maoder Chou

Highlight: A high ceiling balcony connecting both floors' structure.

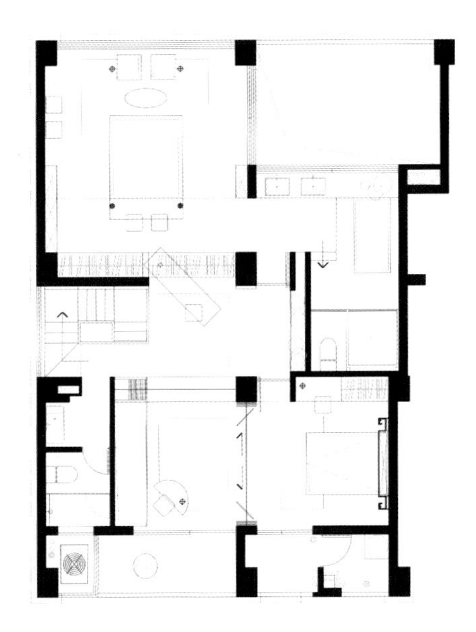
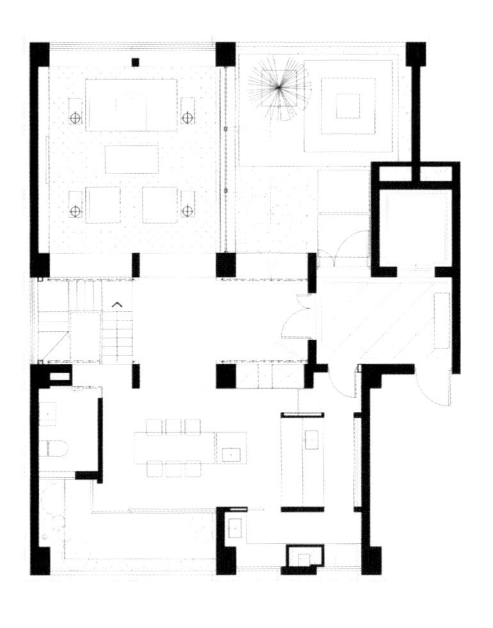

Designers utilise the mirror on the ceiling to enlarge the left and right hidden vertical modelling cabinet in order to connect to and enlarge the focus point of the coloured glaze drop light to the upper and the lower floors.

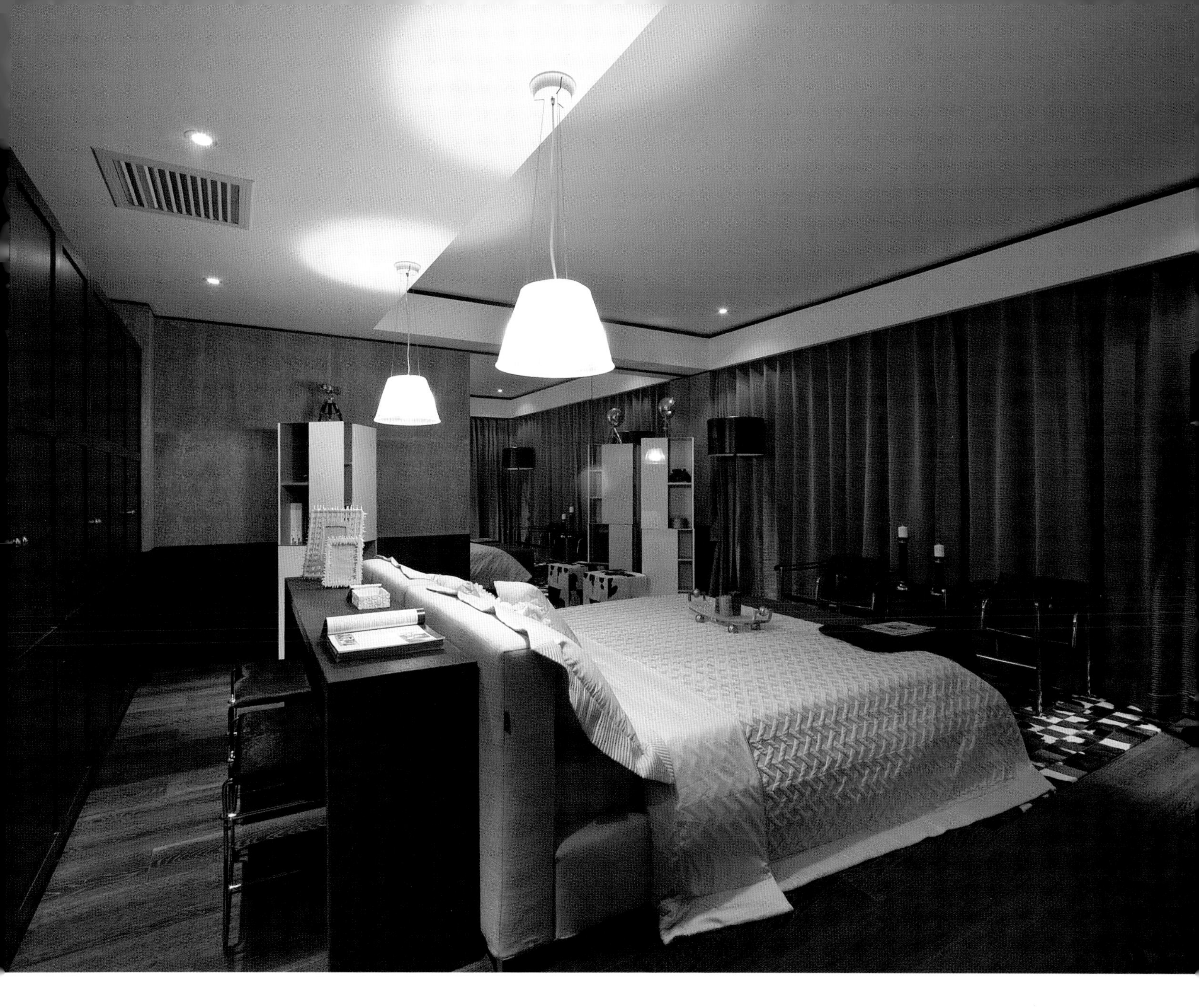

Delano & Collins Suite

The Delano suite covers an area of 102 square metres. Brushed, white-glazed oak flooring; glossy white lacquer cabinetry and fretwork screens; crystal, acrylic, tempered glass and mirrored surfaces create a feeling of sun-washed serenity, while lavender accents add a calming effect. Near the entrance, the small den demonstrates a balance of sleek, contemporary, sumptuous and traditional elements that characterises the South Beach style, with its giant lampshade and crystal pendant light fixture over a glass-topped table; a leather and carved wood chair with nail head detailing; a wall montage of picture-less frames.

In contrast, the 90 square metre Collins suite has been styled in the Hollywood glamour in the later period of South Beach's design history, with a dramatic black and white colour scheme with vivid gold metal accents. Wide charcoal plank wood flooring, mica-like porcelain floor tiles, black lacquer and grey oak cabinets, white marble vanity tops, black granite kitchen countertops, black velvet and leather, grey and white tempered glass are enlivened by surrounding glittering glass tile columns, brass mosaic backsplashes and brushed gold accessories.

Name of Project:
South Beach Condos and Lofts – Model Suites
Location:
Toronto, Canada
Completion Date:
2008
Interior Design:
II BY IV Design Associates Inc.
Dan Menchions,
Keith Rushbrook
Photography:
Joy von Tiedemann

Highlight: These are two model suites among the South Beach condos and lofts.

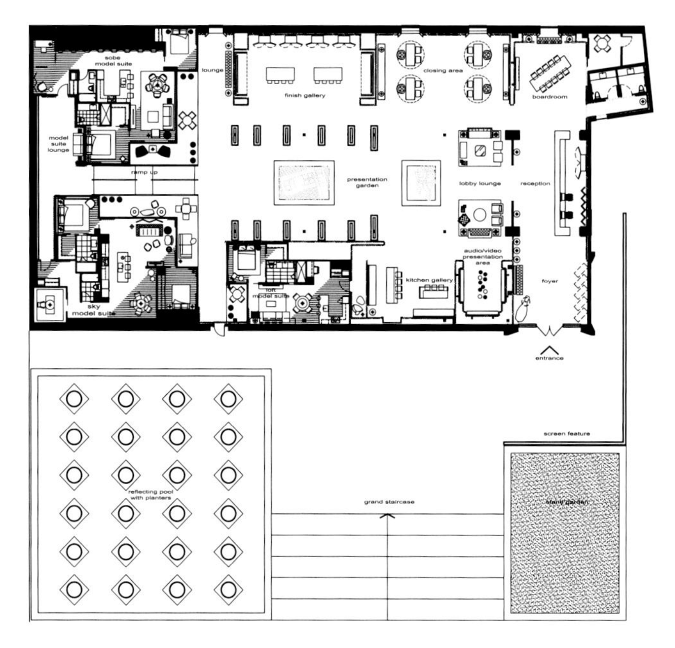
sobe
model suite
lounge
finish gallery
closing area
boardroom
model
suite
lounge
ramp up
presentation
garden
lobby lounge
reception
audio/video
presentation
area
kitchen gallery
foyer
loft
model suite
sky
model suite
entrance
screen feature
reflecting pool
with planters
grand staircase

CONTEMPORARY LIVING

The Collins suite has been styled in the Hollywood glamour in the later period of South Beach's design history, with a dramatic black and white colour scheme with vivid gold metal accents.

Loft Rome

A single space, a global view, and only the colour to distinguish environments. This, in short, is the soul of the project by Barbara Buzi. Opening the large portal here is an overview of a single bright environment, with exposed beams absolutely beyond any concept.

Arranged on two levels connected by side stairs, except for services and the wardrobe, no wall divides the rooms, which are distinguished only by different colour of the walls. Downstairs, two sofas surround a space reserved for the living room, while a huge table and an open kitchen make the dining area warm and familiar. The loft furnishings are unique pieces specially designed and made by InternoB.

The kitchen in "fake" brick (a wooden structure covered) is characterised by a long plane angular and decorations entirely handmade. Upstair is easy to see the light that surrounds the space, darkened if necessary, with a curtain handmade too. The bed, the library cubes and the great dresser complete the furnishings. The bathroom in british green deliberately darkened by the colour choice, gains an atmosphere of relaxation and wellbeing.

Name of Project:
Loft Rome
Location:
Rome, Italy
Completion Date:
2006
Interior Design:
Barbara BUZI - InternoB
Photography:
Catinofoto.com

Highlight: A single space, a global view, and only the colour to distinguish environments.

Opening the large portal here is an overview of a single bright environment, with exposed beams absolutely beyond any concept.

No rules, no brands, but only imagination and personalised creations for an absolutely exclusive home.

Tribeca Penthouse

Questioning balance in this open-concept penthouse, the main objective was to create a flexible, intimate living space with the expansive views. The apartment exudes the feel of a well-designed ship sailing out over the Hudson River.

The client, a successful executive, requested complete privacy for his living quarters on the top floor, roomy accommodations for guests below, and free access to the roof terrace. The use of lavish materials with their varied textures reflects the owner's South American roots as well as the designer's taste for modern yet classic interiors. The blueprint and structural characteristics of this beautiful space brought serious limitations. In order to meet the client's needs; the original staircase was relocated to the middle of the two-storey space, allowing the installation of a second full bath on the first floor.

The custom-designed spiral staircase from Italy is compact and airy, appearing to float rather than obstructing the view. With the long south wall of the window came the challenge of maintaining a comfortable temperature throughout the seasons. The designer combined a split unit system with simple floor heating, both coordinated with electric shades and controlled by a sophisticated AV system.

Name of Project:
Tribeca Penthouse
Location:
Manhattan, USA
Completion Date:
2009
Interior Design:
Modo Design,
Jesus Garza
Photography:
Mikiko Kikuyama
Client:
Anonymous

Highlight: The apartment exudes the feel of a well-designed ship sailing out over the Hudson River.

The custom-designed spiral staircase from Italy is compact and airy, appearing to float rather than obstructing the view.

HAUTE SPACES: RESIDENCES
The Book and All Seamless Patterns Created by Dopress (www.dopress.com).
Copyright © 2011 Dopress Ltd. All Rights Reserved.

210-309 VILLA+HOUSE
Haute Spaces: Residences

Tierney Watson

The client was very inspired by Mid Century "Palm Springs" design from the USA West Coast, which essentially added a layer of playful decoration over Modernist construction methods. Council requirements called for a "traditional" cottage scale from the streetscape, but from there on the design was free to flow to a more relaxed, resort-like quality towards the rear of the property.

The look fused very Australian elements with a European sensibility. This sensibility was shared with the US who in the 1950's created new and more interesting forms with very modern building methods. The design of this house is homage to these principles. The traditional and kitsch elements have been contemporized to create a very modern house. The strong elements of the building are echoed in the soft furnishes creating a one harmonious whole.

The warm tones of the neutrals of the hard architectural elements such as the greys and beiges of the travertine flooring, the stained oak and the grey concrete as well as the pure white walls and details act as a backdrop to the applied colour of the furnishings. The furniture and soft architectural details add a touch of whimsical colour to an otherwise austere scheme.

Name Of Project:
Tierney Watson House
Location:
Balmain, Australia
Completion Date:
2010
Interior Design:
Greg Natale Design.
Greg Natale,
Victor Wong,
Stewart Horton
Photography:
Anson Smart
Client:
Michelle Tierney,
Craig Watson

Highlight: The traditional and kitsch elements have been contemporized to create a very modern house.

ROBUCHON

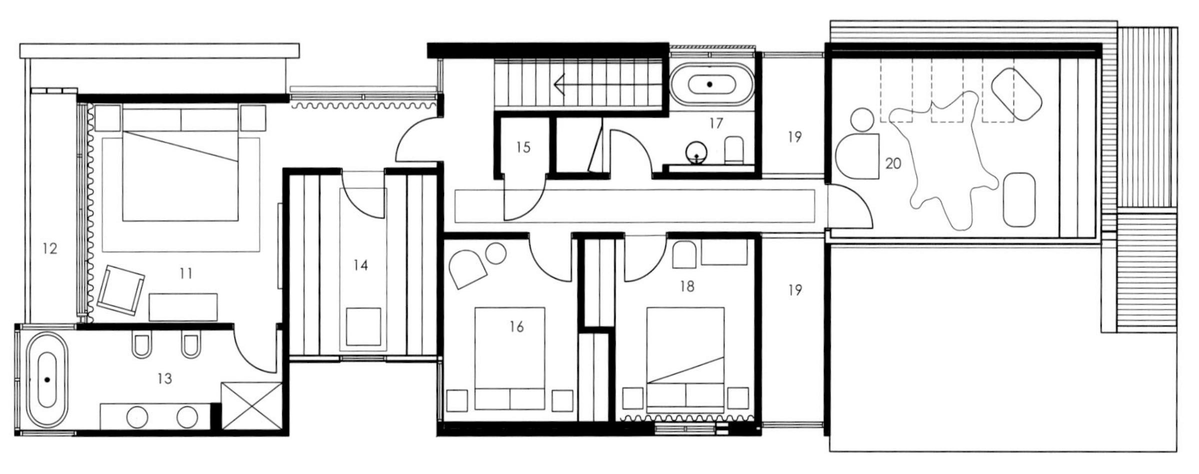
17
15
19
20
12
11
14
18
19
16
13

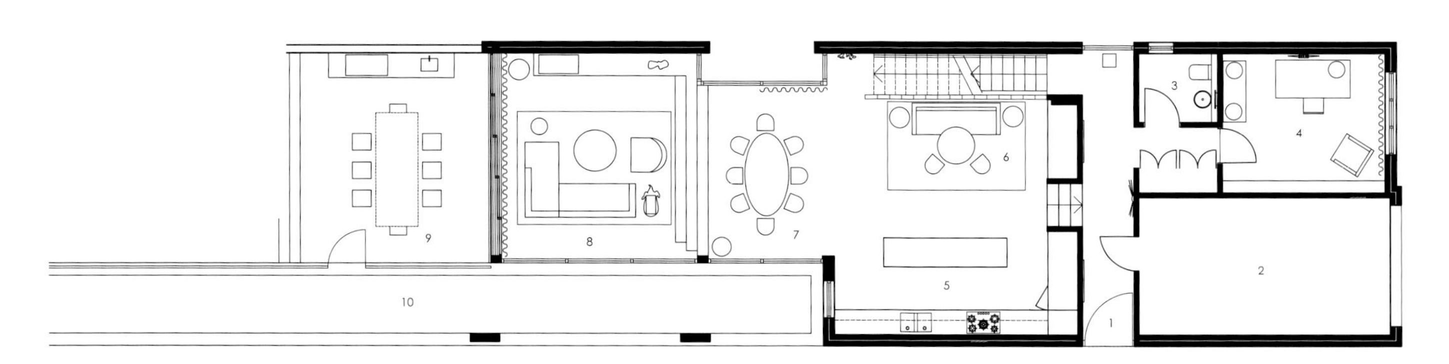
3
4
6
9
8
7
2
10
5
1

A very important element in the design is the linking of the geometric concrete besser walls which act as room dividers and privacy screens. These walls were left raw to enable the grey colour to help tie in other elements such as the silver travertine.

M
C

The warm tones of the neutrals of the hard architectural elements such as the greys and beiges of the travertine flooring, the stained oak and the grey concrete as well as the pure white walls and details act as a backdrop to the applied colour of the furnishings.

INVOGUE

Greenwich Village

The residence was completely renovated and will function as the client's Pied-a-terre. The living area features multiple patterns and textures, and an eclectic collection of furniture and art pieces. There is a silk rug in warm tones with a herringbone pattern by Fort Street Studio and a custom designed sofa in crushed velvet. The ottoman is from Ralph Pucci and it is covered with a subtle floral pattern. An ox blood leather lounge and a Brazilian wood chair and saddle leather complete the seating group.

The room is separated by sliding panels of glass with a chrome ink mirrored interlayer that fades to clear – providing both light and privacy for the space. Outside of the den is the client's wenge lacquer art deco desk with recessed bronze metal shelving for books, objects and small photos.

A vintage mid-century floor lamp, a chair by Jean Nouvel, and ottomans by Milo Baumann compose the seating area in the bedroom. Connecting the dressing area and bath is a hall of patterned wall covering reminiscent of a Sol LeWitt design.

Name of Project:
Greenwich Village Residence
Location:
New York, USA
Completion Date:
2009
Interior Design:
Janson Goldstein LLP
Photography:
Mikiko Kikuyama

Highlight: The plan is open and the spaces flow together with little separation between functions.

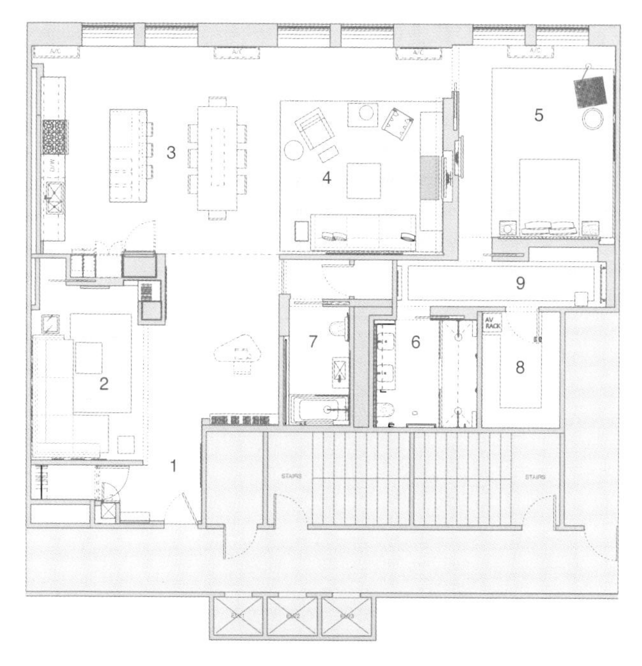
3
4
5
9
7
6
8
AV RACK
2
1
STAIRS
STAIRS

The living area features multiple patterns and textures, and an eclectic collection of furniture and art pieces. There is a silk rug in warm tones with a herringbone pattern by Fort Street Studio and a custom designed sofa in crushed velvet.

The island provides additional cooking and storage capabilities and of course a place to gather around. Adjacent to the island is the oversized dining table in natural walnut with bronze detailing. The chairs are oil quenched metal frames with leather straps; above is a bronze crystal chandelier by Swarovski.

A vintage mid-century floor lamp, a chair by Jean Nouvel, and ottomans by Milo Baumann compose the seating area in the bedroom.

The "N" House

The tropical climate is taken as a main consideration to drive the architectural geometry concept, along with the material chosen.

Inside the modern building of tropical Asian architecture style, they try to put 'traditional' interior element, like semi transparent wall partition in the family room, to soften the atmosphere. A piece of natural wood is used as a dining table accompany to give a warm feeling to this area as a "main heart" of this residence.

In master bathroom, they try to elaborate the "gallery" concept, with the rectilinear space arrangement, which maximizes the natural daylight through the gap between the room and the perimeter wall. The colour and material palette use the earth, creamy colour contrasting with dark, aged and rustic wood appearance.

Name of Project:
The "N" House
Location:
Jakarta, Indonesia
Completion Date:
2008
Interior Design:
TWS & Partners,
Tonny Wirawan Suriadjaja
Architectural Design:
TWS & Partners
Photography:
Tectography,
Fernando Gomulya

Highlight: The tropical climate is taken as a main consideration to drive the architectural geometry concept.

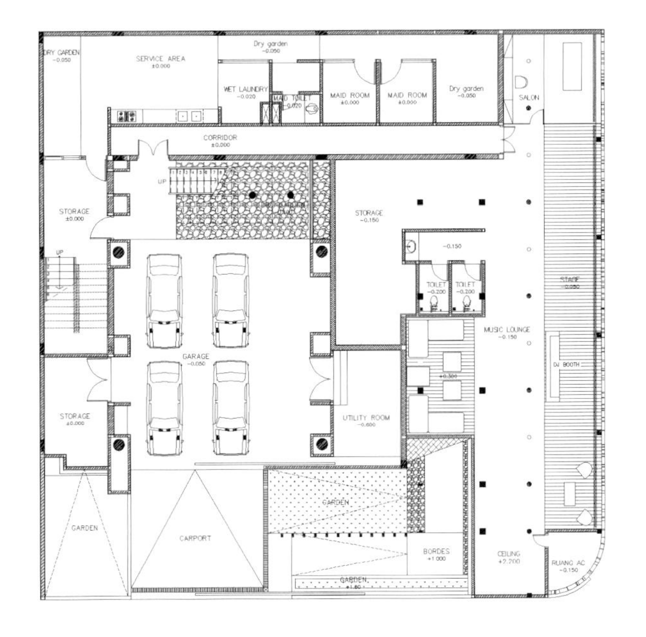
DRY GARDEN
-0.050
SERVICE AREA
±0.000
Dry garden
-0.050
WET LAUNDRY
-0.020
MAID TOILET
-0.020
MAID ROOM
±0.000
MAID ROOM
±0.000
Dry garden
-0.050
SALON
CORRIDOR
±0.000
UP
STORAGE
±0.000
STORAGE
-0.150
-0.150
UP
TOILET
-0.200
TOILET
-0.200
STAGE
MUSIC LOUNGE
-0.150
GARAGE
-0.050
DJ BOOTH
+0.300
STORAGE
±0.000
UTILITY ROOM
-0.600
GARDEN
GARDEN
CARPORT
BORDES
+1.000
CEILING
+2.200
RUANG AC
-0.150
GARDEN
+1.80

In master bathroom, they try to elaborate the "gallery" concept, with the rectilinear space arrangement, which maximizes the natural daylight through the gap between the room and the perimeter wall.

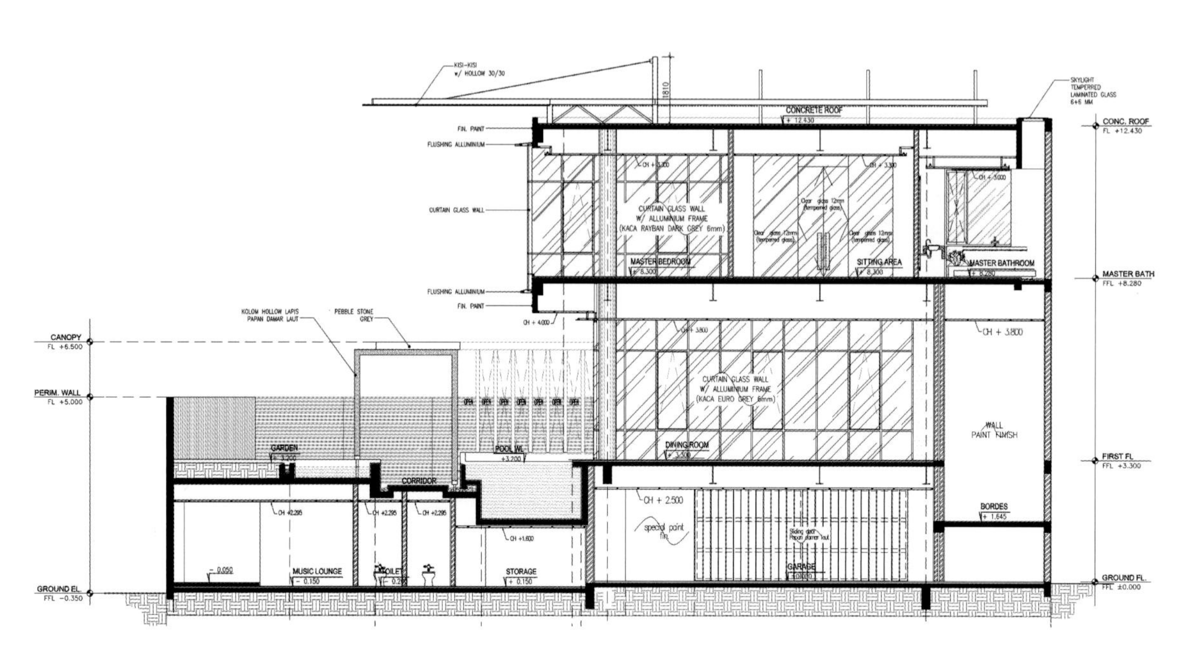
KISI-KISI
w/ HOLLOW 30/30
FIN. PAINT
FLUSHING ALLUMINIUM
CURTAIN GLASS WALL
FLUSHING ALLUMINIUM
FIN. PAINT
CH + 4.000
KOLOM HOLLOW LAPIS
PAPAN DAMAR LAUT
PEBBLE STONE
GREY
CANOPY
FL +6.500
PERIM. WALL
FL +5.000
GARDEN
POOL WL
+3.200
CORRIDOR
CH +2.295
CH +2.295
CH +2.295
CH +1.600
- 0.050
MUSIC LOUNGE
- 0.150
STORAGE
+ 0.150
GROUND EL.
FFL -0.350
1810
CONCRETE ROOF
+ 12.430
SKYLIGHT
TEMPERRED
LAMINATED GLASS
6+6 MM
CONC. ROOF
FL +12.430
CH + 3.300
CH + 3.300
CH + 3.000
CURTAIN GLASS WALL
W/ ALLUMINIUM FRAME
(KACA RAYBAN DARK GREY 6mm)
Clear glass 12mm
(tempered glass)
MASTER BEDROOM
+ 8.300
SITTING AREA
+ 8.300
MASTER BATHROOM
+ 8.280
MASTER BATH
FFL +8.280
CH + 3.800
CH + 3.800
CURTAIN GLASS WALL
W/ ALLUMINIUM FRAME
(KACA EURO GREY 6mm)
WALL
PAINT FINISH
DINING ROOM
+ 3.300
FIRST FL
FFL +3.300
CH + 2.500
special paint
fin.
GARAGE
±0.000
BORDES
+ 1.645
GROUND FL.
FFL ±0.000

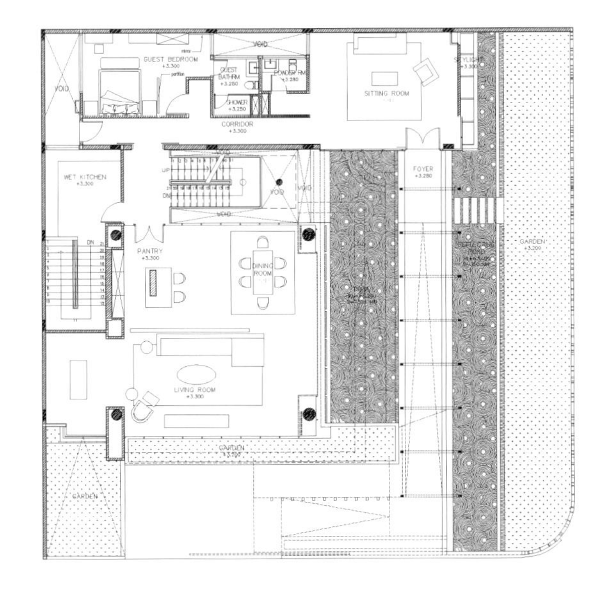
VOID
GUEST BEDROOM
+3.300
GUEST
BATHRM
+3.280
POWDER RM
+3.280
SHOWER
+3.250
SITTING ROOM
SKYLIGHT
+3.300
CORRIDOR
+3.300
WET KITCHEN
+3.300
UP
DN
FOYER
+3.280
PANTRY
+3.300
DINING
ROOM
GARDEN
+3.200
LIVING ROOM
+3.300
GARDEN
+3.100
GARDEN

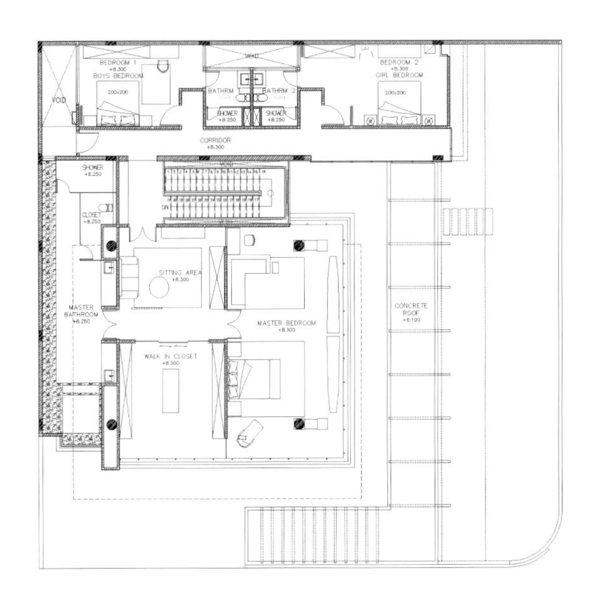
BEDROOM 1
+8.300
BOYS BEDROOM
200x200
VOID
BATHRM
BATHRM 2
SHOWER
+8.250
SHOWER
+8.250
BEDROOM 2
+8.300
GIRL BEDROOM
200x200
CORRIDOR
+8.300
SHOWER
+8.250
CLOSET
+8.250
DN
SITTING AREA
+8.300
MASTER
BATHROOM
+8.280
MASTER BEDROOM
+8.300
WALK IN CLOSET
+8.300
CONCRETE
ROOF
+6.100

Log Cabin Hafjell

To create a warm atmosphere with a modern interior design concept, the expression is rooted in warm shades of gray. Both wooden floors and log walls are treated with special coloured stain, specially made for this project and client.

The entrance hall is spacious and has a magnificent ceiling. The height in the hallway and the bedroom wing is perfect for the three modern and transparent lamps. Kitchen furniture is specially designed and built on site, stained in a dark and warm blackish gray tone without visible grip, so the expression becomes functional, but still modern. Kitchen and dining room was designed as a family room with a small workspace and a bar. The furniture in the dining room consists of a specially designed heavy wooden table that is light grey stained and sleek dining chairs in leather.

The living room is a step lower and has a wonderful view over the valley and Gubrandsdalen. Earth-coloured fabrics and carpets, patterned cushions, combined with some leather give a warm but clean mountain feel.

Name of Project:
Log Cabin Hafjell
Location:
Hafjell 2636 Øyer, Norway
Completion Date:
2008
Interior Design:
AS Scenario Interiørarkiteter MNIL
Photography:
Mona Gundersen

Highlight: A warm atmosphere with a modern interior design concept.

7950
V1
V1
V2
V2
V1
V1
KØYE-SENG
Sov 1
Sov 2
KØYE-SENG
Badstu
3,8 m2
3000
Bad2
13,2 m2
Vask/bod
4,4 m2
ARB.PLASS
RETNING PLANK
Kjøkken
Bad1
3,9 m2
2750
Garderobe
4,6 m2
3400
7400
RETNING PLANK
TV-stue
1200
3900
Konsollbord m/speil
900
V3
Entre
20,2 m2
1220
Sov 3
13,9 m2
ca 600
Peis
RETNING PLANK
11900
V5
RETNING PLANK
D3
V4
V4
4200
V4
V1
V4
V1
Stue
D2
TREGULV
BRASILIANSK SKIFER

Earth-coloured fabrics and carpets, patterned cushions, combined with some leather give a warm but clean mountain feel throughout the living room .

Kitchen furniture is specially designed and built on site, stained in a dark and warm blackish gray tone without visible grip, so the expression becomes functional, but still modern.

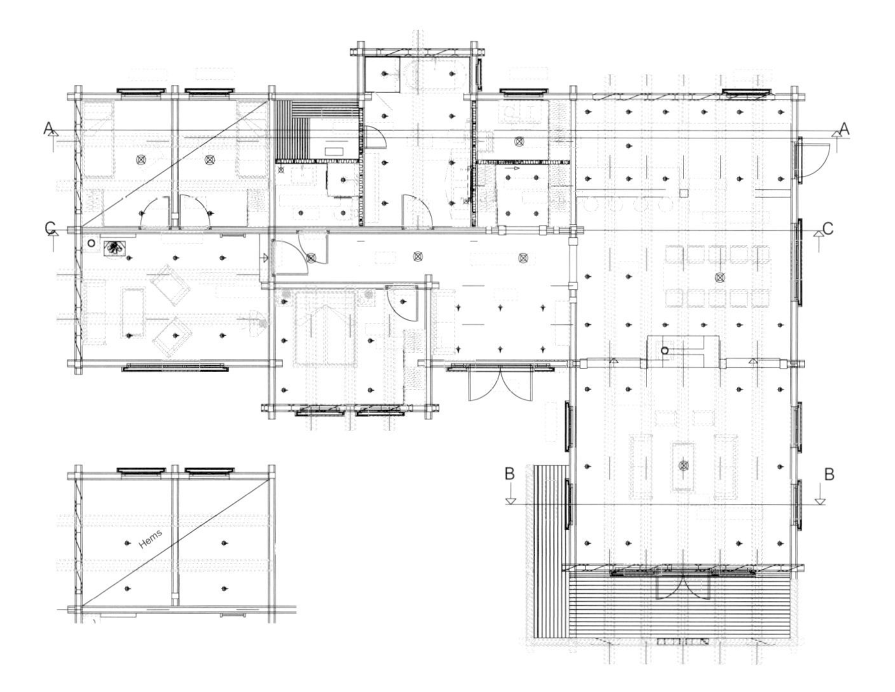
A
A
C
C
B
B
Hems

Villa No.10

Aged Chinese architectural concept is fully presented in the project. On the left side of the space there is living area, and the other side the dining area and kitchen. The hallway maximized natural light and created elegant atmosphere with the decoration of bamboo.

On the 2nd floor, designers adopted open and closed design concept to make the bathroom spacious but private, breaking the limitness of the original structure.

The usage of shell panel as the background of the master bed adds a sense of fanciness to the master bedroom on the 3rd floor. The carp painting on the entrance door of the dressing room lends fascination. On the other side of the room there is interior study connected directly to bathroom.

Basement is designed to meet the entertainment need of the client, the big room functions as the room of wine keeping, wine tasting and meeting friends.

Name of Project:
Villa No.10
Location:
Shanghai, China
Completion Date:
2010
Interior Design:
Mohen Design International,
Hank M.Chao,
Zhao lu
Photography:
Mohen Design International,
Maoder Chou

Highlight: Aged Chinese architectural concept is fully presented in the project.

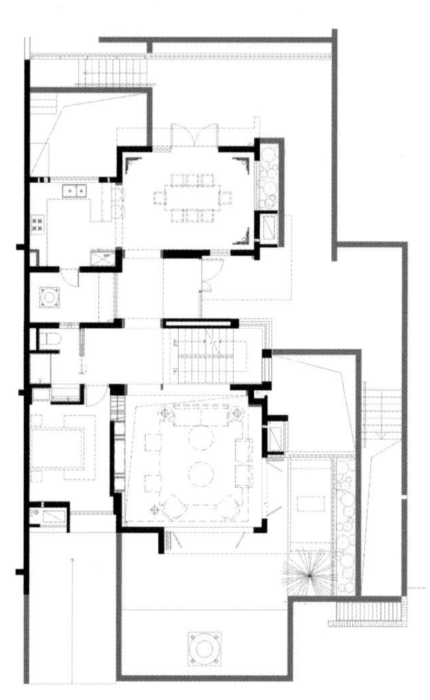

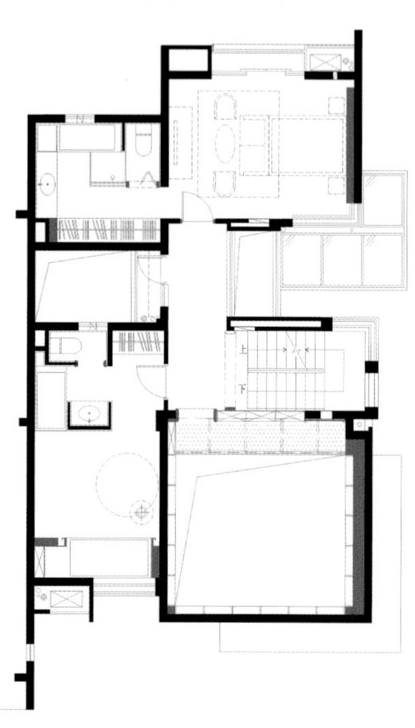

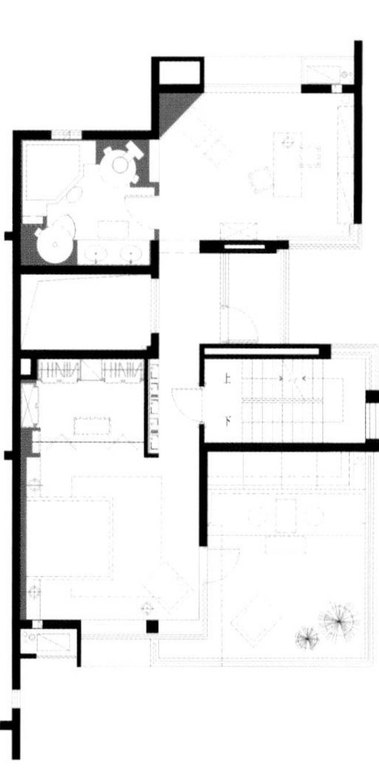

Residence "C"

Located in one of the most exclusive residential developments in Mexico City, an important achievement of this project was to create a sophisticated, familiar and warm ambience.

Material used recalls the luxury in mansions and villas. In the living room a beige and pale blues palette created bright and soft contrasts. The dinning room displayed an oval ceiling panel with mahogany wooden planks, similar to the access foyer. The kitchen is one of the most spectacular areas, it is custom-made and fabricated in mahogany wood. A table, placed all along the center, brings the opportunity to have pleasant reunions. The master bedroom includes a living room, a complete equipped gym, massage room, marble steam room. Colour scheme is warm and luminous, carefully selected in order to harmonize with furniture and curtains.

This eclectic decoration combines antiques and contemporary and classical furnishings. Most of the lamps and furniture were exclusively designed by Pascal Arquitectos for this residence.

Name Of Project:
Residence "C"
Location:
Mexico City, Mexico
Completion Date:
2010
Interior Design:
Pascal Arquitectos
Carlos Pascal
Gerard Pascal
Photography:
Jaime Navarro

Highlight: Material used recalls the luxury in mansions and villas.

Breakfast room
Dining room
Kitchen
Terrace
Main access
Foyer
Terrace
Living room

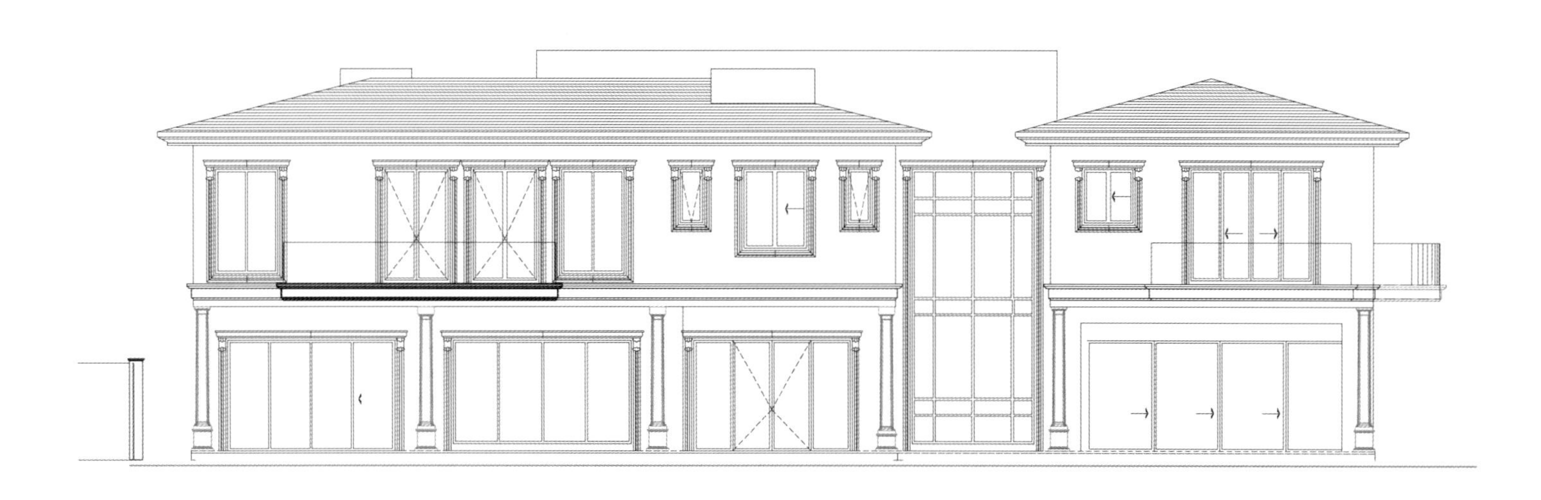

The kitchen is one of the most spectacular areas, it is custom-made and fabricated in mahogany wood.

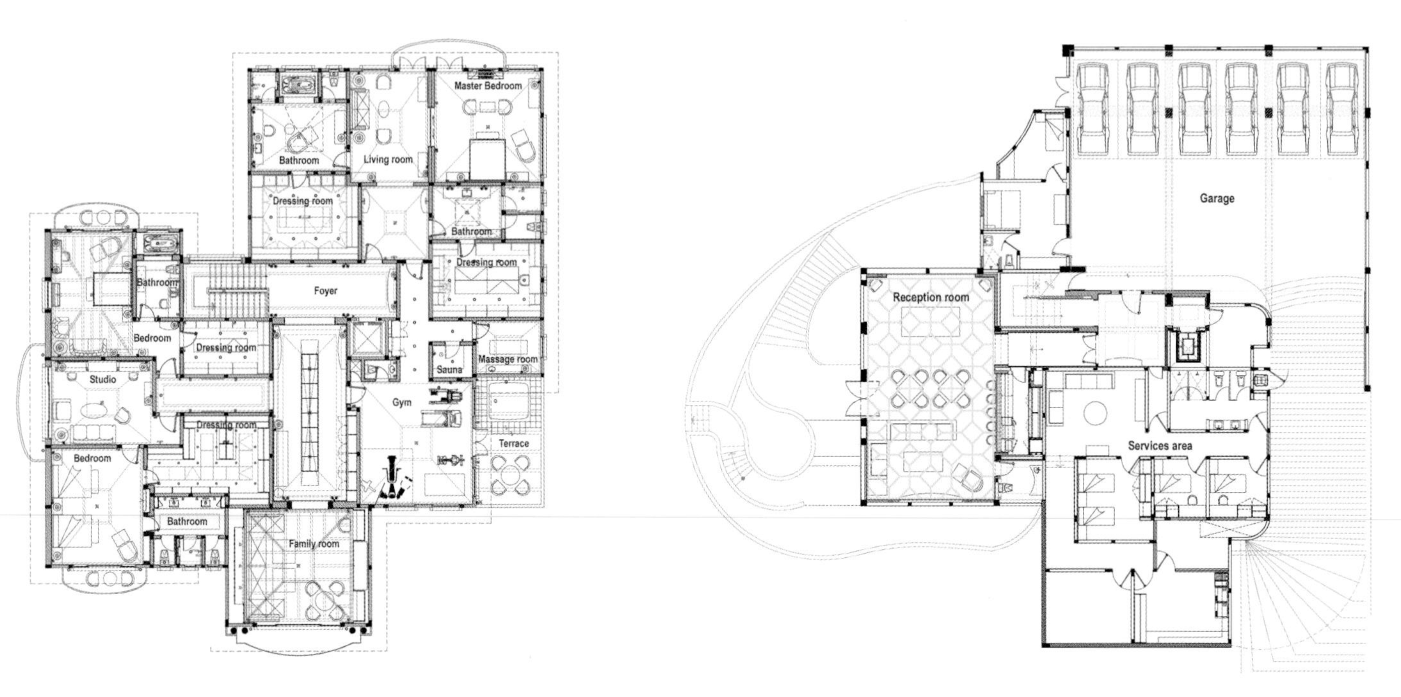
Master Bedroom
Bathroom
Living room
Dressing room
Bathroom
Bathroom
Dressing room
Foyer
Bedroom
Dressing room
Sauna
Massage room
Studio
Gym
Dressing room
Terrace
Bedroom
Bathroom
Family room
Garage
Reception room
Services area

In the living room a beige and pale blues palette created bright and soft contrasts.

Casa Son Vida

Casa is an example of design poetry in motion. The completion of this remarkable home marks the arrival of third millennia architecture on the island of Mallorca. The task at hand was straightforward: take a very un-extraordinary existing Mediterranean villa constructed in the 60's and transform it into something extraordinary. The 800 square meters luxury villa transgresses the constraints of site and context, redefining luxury architecture as it is typified by the traditional and prolific Mediterranean and Tuscan styles otherwise found on the island.

The building that houses Casa Son Vida is composed of an old and a new part. The stunning architecture (by Tec ARCHITECTURE) of the new extension inspired Marcel Wanders to complement the building with a highly exclusive, captivating interior design, perfectly linking old and new. The round and square shapes, soft blobs and new antiques create a unity of the architecture and the interior design.

A mix of traditional and modern references is visible throughout the villa, from the classical profiled wall lining the curved space to the newly custom designed cupboards in straight lines. All aspects of the space and dimensions are played with by using relief and contrasting smooth surfaces, creating a unique and artistic atmosphere.

Name of Project:
Casa Son Vida
Location:
Palma De Mallorca, Spain
Completion Date:
2009
Developer:
Cosmopolitan Estates
Interior Design:
Marcel Wanders
Photography:
Marcel Wanders Studio,
Gaelle Le Boulicault

Highlight: An example of design poetry in motion.

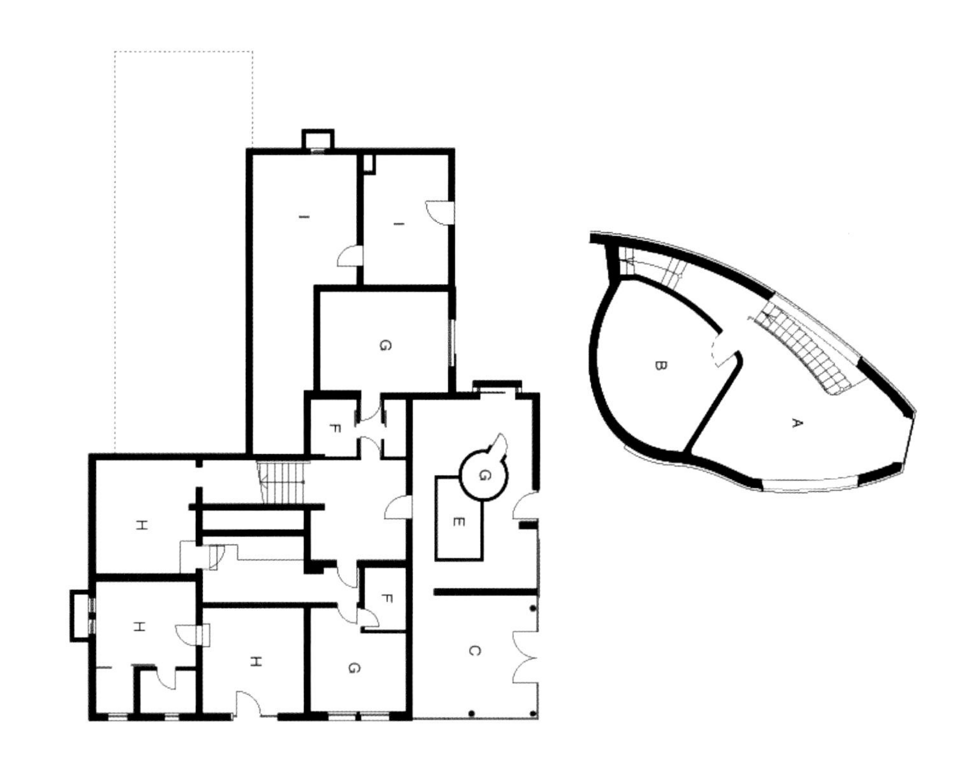

I
I
G
F
G
E
H
H
F
H
C
G
B
A

The new antiques, custom floral patterns wallpaper, bright red sofa and the custom designed cupboards, all bring amazing and luxury style throughout the villa.

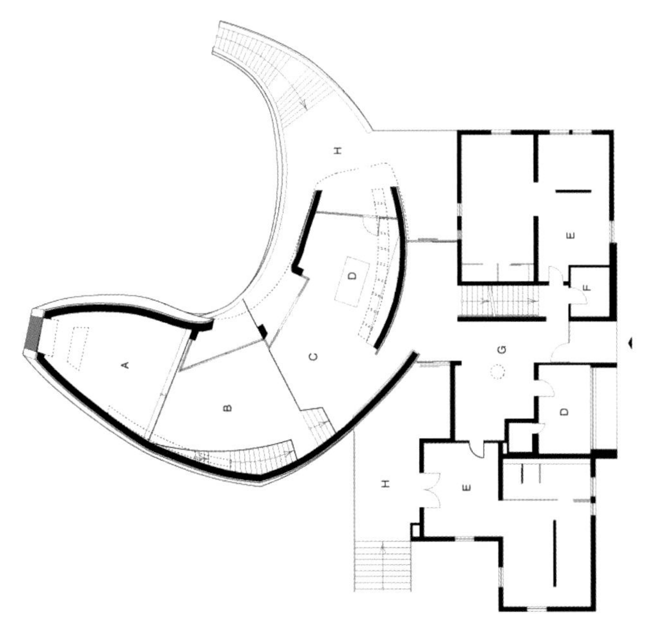

H
E
D
F
A
C
G
B
D
H
E

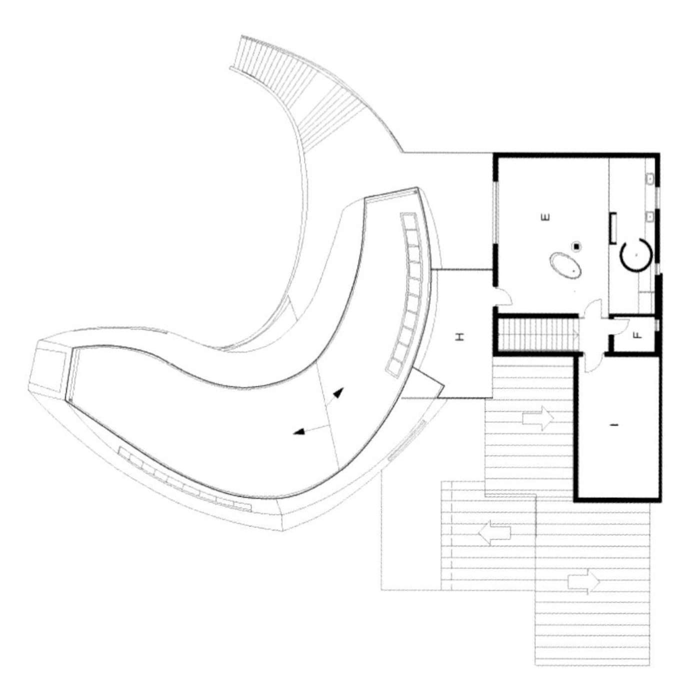
E
H
F
I

Casa Son Vida 2

Adjacent to the original Villa is Casa Son Vida 2, which is a pared-down, simplified box structure. This 600 square meters home makes the most of its secluded and private setting on a large private plot. The least avant garde of the Platinum Estates villas, this modern home is nonetheless a departure from the typical Mediterranean homes that abound on the island.

Traditional boundaries are blurred in this rectilinear house with spaces flowing seamlessly between indoor and out. A master suite perches above the large pool allowing endless views across the surrounding hill tops. Structurally a box, this residence is anything but square.

Name of Project:
Casa Son Vida 2
Location:
Palma De Mallorca, Spain
Completion Date:
2009
Developer:
Cosmopolitan Estates
Interior Design:
Marcel Wanders
Photography:
Heidi Warth

Highlight: Traditional boundaries are blurred in this rectilinear house.

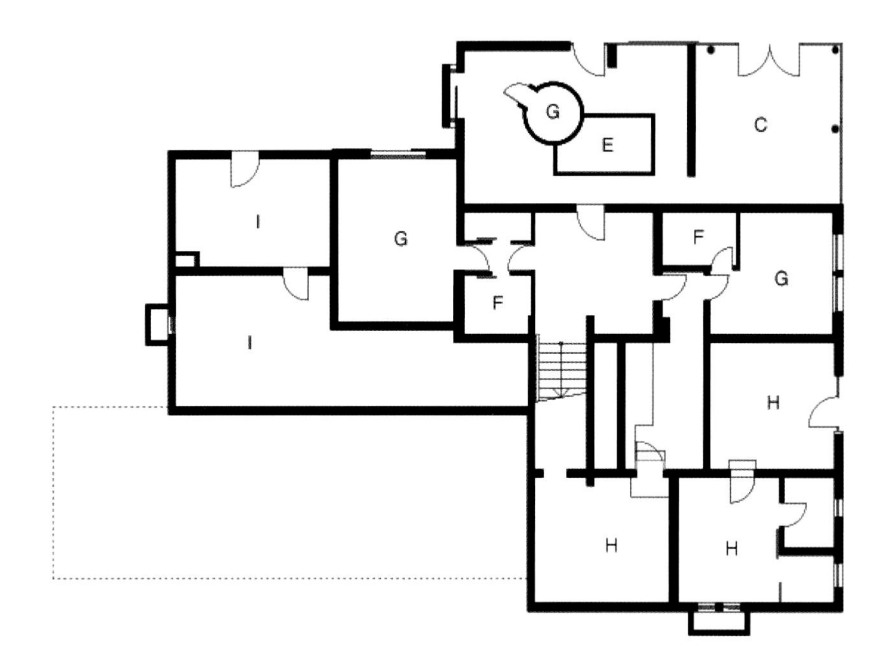
G
E
C
I
G
F
F
G
I
H
H
H

The Buddha wall painting in the bedroom and living room add a religionary art atmosphere.

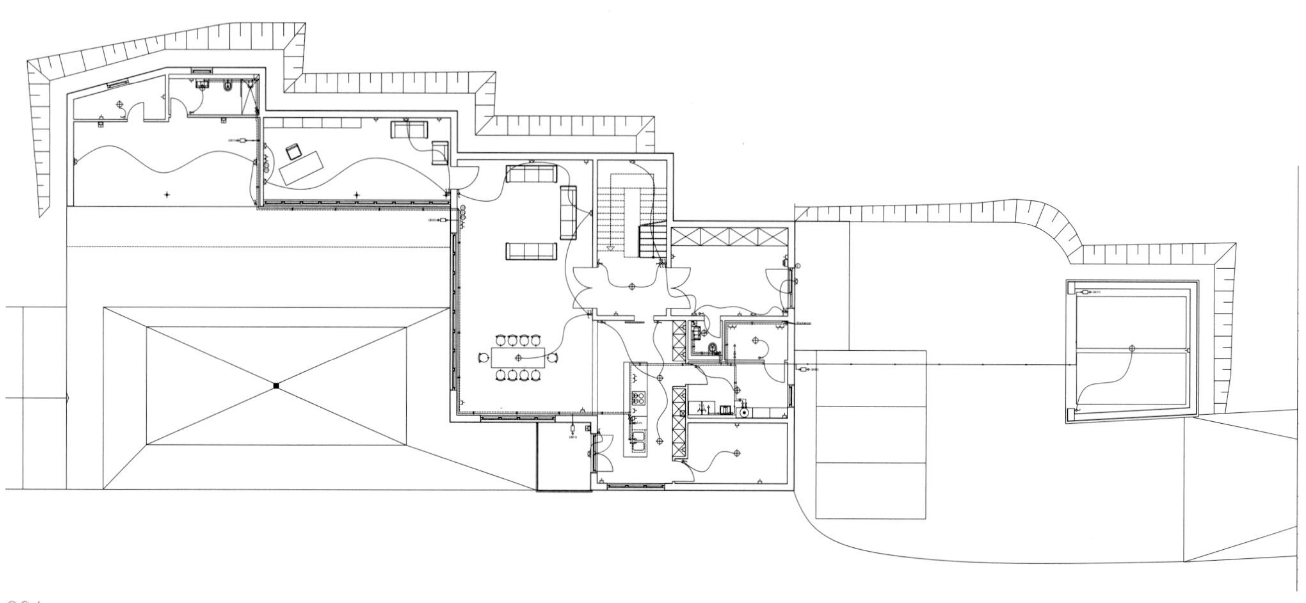

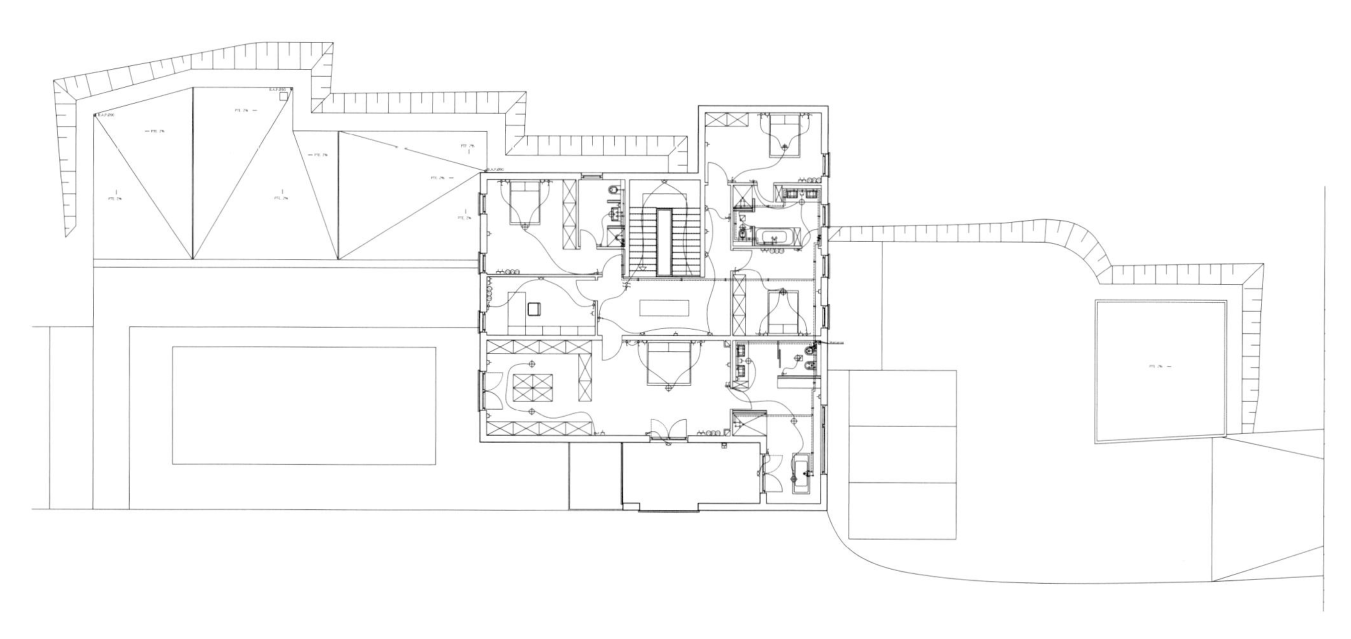

Buama House

BUAMA is an interior project for a young couple living in Beykoz. The smooth and endless lines are associated with infinity. The scattering of light on the new surface also reminds you of limitlessness.

The furniture is chosen to bring different styles together. The couple have some beautiful antique pieces, so they want to combine the new furniture with them. Those pieces catch the attention over the white and smooth walls and ceilings.

The garden is also designed on the same infinite principle. The lines seem endless. Between the existing trees a resting place is designed. This calming, quiet and relaxing green space will be a place where the couple will enjoy their free time.

Name of Project:
Buama House
Location:
Beykoz, Turkey
Completion Date:
2009
Interior Design:
Global Architectural Development,
Gokhan Avcioglu,
Muge Tan,
Caglar Temizyurek
Photography:
Caglar Temizyurek,
Ozlem Avcioglu
Client:
Beyza Uyanoglu

Highlight: The furniture is chosen to bring different styles together.

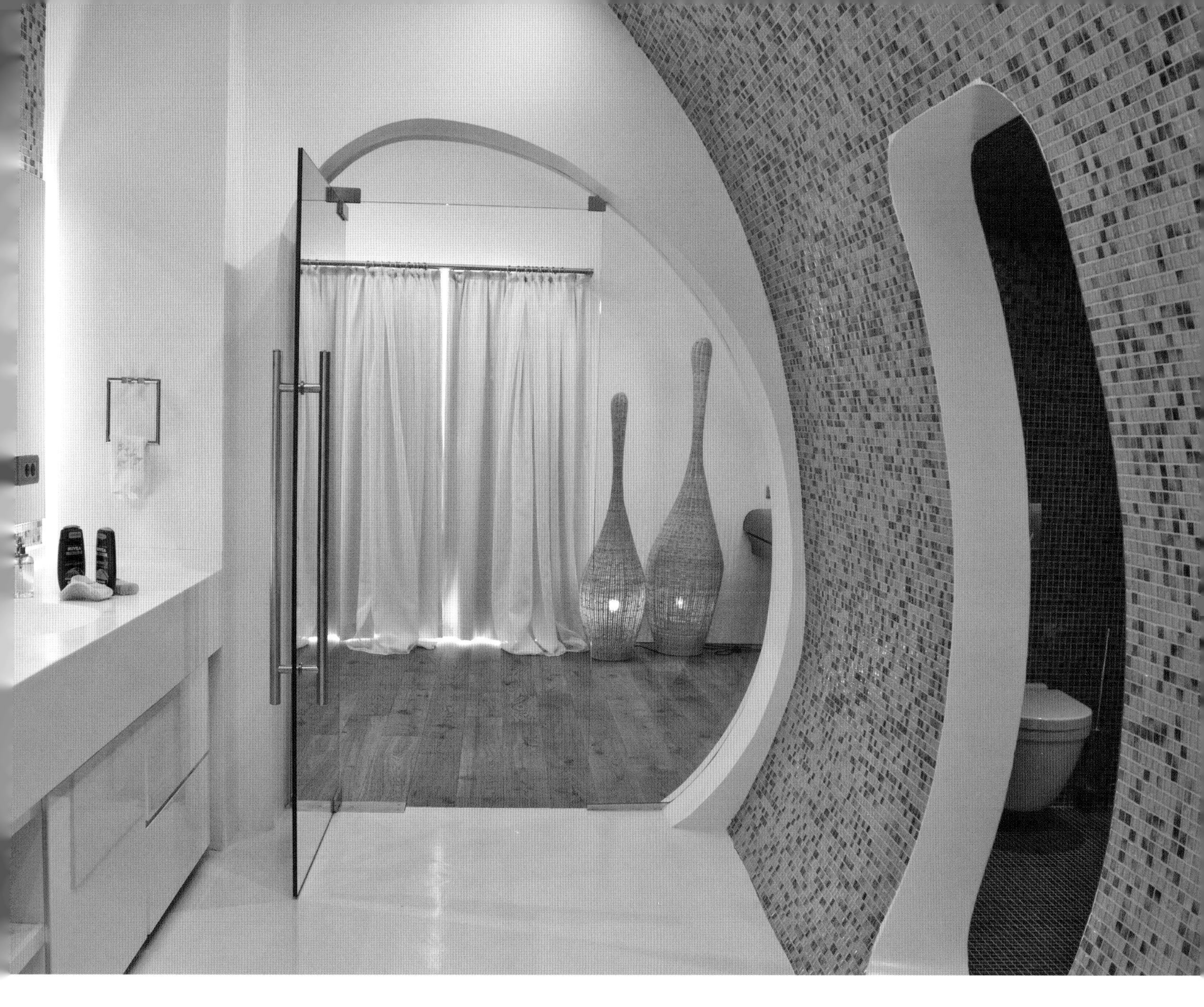

The smooth and endless lines are in anarc and associated with infinity. The scattering of light on the new surface also reminds you of limitlessness.

Amazing Villa G

Villa G lies like a white landmark in the soft landscape at Hjellestad, near Bergen. The house is large yet not dominating, modern but not pretentious. The house has a futuristic form but is built with traditional Nordic materials and architectural elements with a good basis in Norwegian building methods.

The architect and the client started out on good terms and ended up having a very good working collaboration in all stages of the project. The architect liked the larger lines while the client was a perfectionist in regards to the details. The process was very symbiotic.

The stair for example was developed together with the client and evolved after at least 10-12 suggestion that ended up as this final stair. The stair is one solid piece of 1cm thick steel, galvanised with white sand corn making it slip resistant. The stair is produced locally, weighs almost a tonne, and had to be lifted into place by a crane through the window in the roof.

Name of Project:
Villa G
Location:
Bergen, Norway
Completion Date:
2009
Interior Design:
Todd Saunders
Photography:
Todd Saunders

Highlight: The house has a futuristic form but is built with traditional Nordic materials and architectural elements.

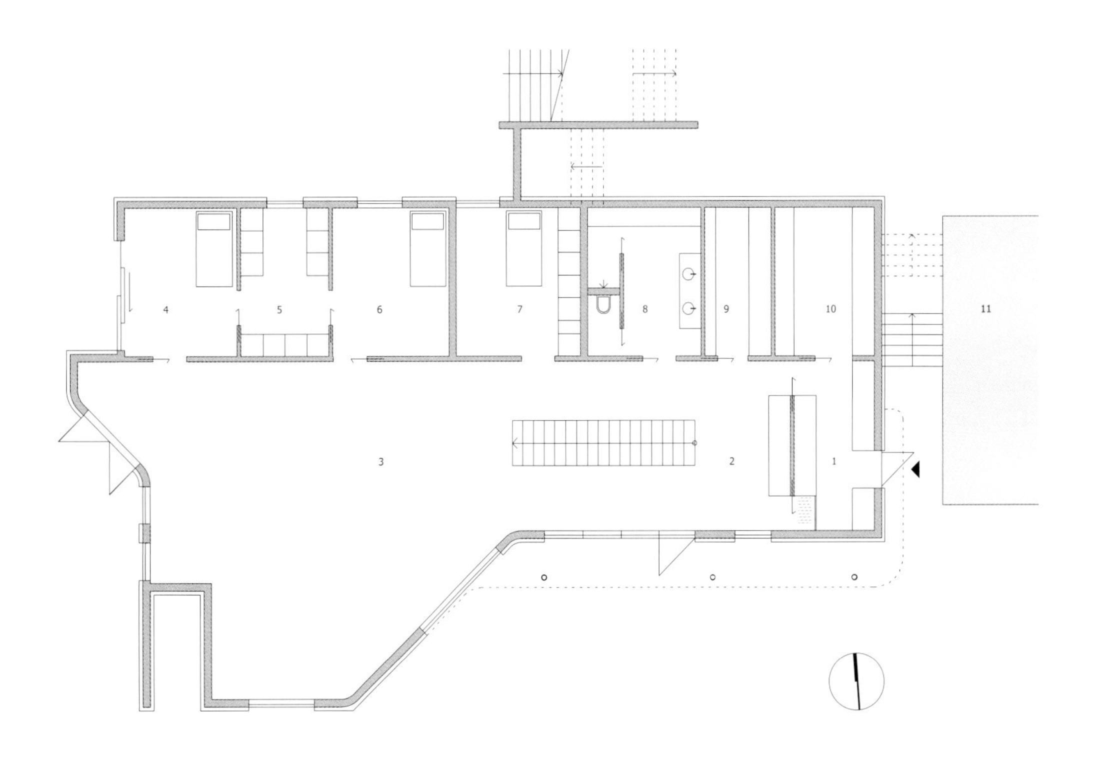
4
5
6
7
8
9
10
11
3
2
1

The stair is one solid piece of 1cm thick steel, galvanised with white sand corn making it slip resistant. The stair is produced locally, weighs almost a tonne, and had to be lifted into place by a crane through the window in the roof.

Hillside House

Built on an infill lot close to town, the house is designed to maximize solar orientation for the photovoltaic panels, as well as passive heating and cooling. The surrounding hillside provides the lower floors with natural insulation, solar power supplies electricity and hot water, and radiant floor heating and an innovative air re-circulation system condition the interior. The home is equipped with whole-house automation and lighting system, LED lighting, Fleetwood super-insulated doors and windows and indigenous, drought-tolerant landscaping to conserve resources.

Materials include sustainably harvested floors and cabinetry from Plantation Hardwoods and New World Millworks, reclaimed timber and recycled metal roofing. Design elements crafted locally from reclaimed materials, such as hand-crafted tile from Sausalito-based Heath Ceramics and steelwork from artist Brian Kennedy, give the project deep roots in the community, making it sustainable from a community standpoint.

Every inch of this LEED Platinum custom home has been designed to maximize its sustainability, in direct response to the site, trees and views. Consequently, this home lives far larger than its actual footprint, but with an impact that is far less.

Name of Project:
The Hillside House
Location:
Mill Valley, USA
Completion Date:
2010
Interior Design:
SB Architects
Photography:
Mariko Reed
Client:
Tracy&Scott Lee

Highlight: Every inch of this LEED Platinum custom home has been designed to maximize its sustainability.

CALATRAVA

SCOTT
TRACY
CAMERON

Waterbirds

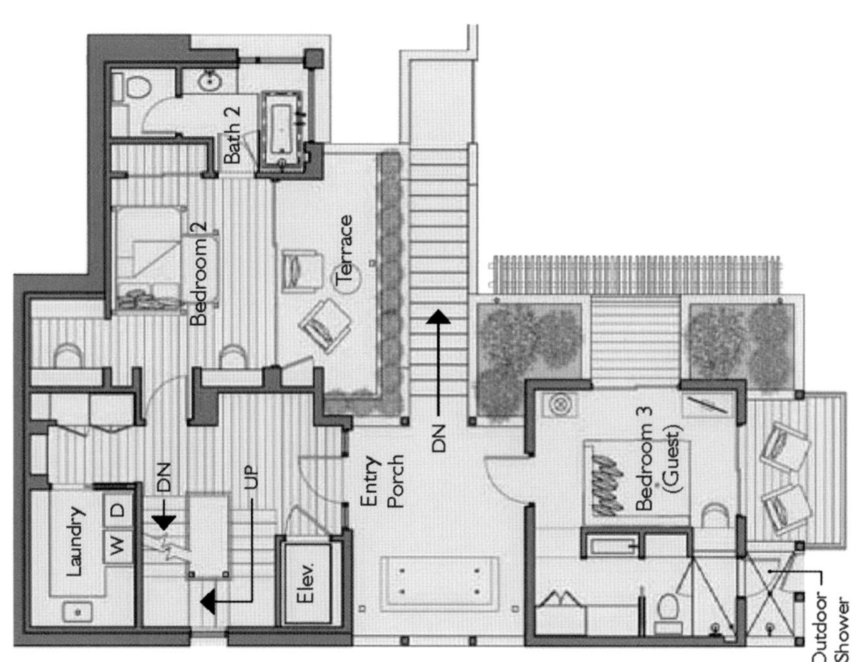

"An important part of minimizing the impact of a project involves selecting products, like Western Red Cedar, that minimize the carbon footprint from manufacture to end use," says Scott Lee.

Abelow Sherman

Add: 330 West 38th Street, Suite 1100 New York, NY 10018, USA
Tel: 212-627-8866
Web: www.abelowsherman.com

Abelow Sherman Architects LLC is a uniquely attentive architectural firm based in New York City. In this practice the two partners, David Abelow and David Sherman are personally very involved in every project, limiting the amount of commissions that can be accepted at any one time. The staff consists of seven highly talented architects and designers who have worked together for many years, and have diverse resumes pre-dating their arrival at Abelow Sherman. Most of the staff have been with the firm for eight years or more, enjoying the responsibility, professionalism and collegial environment. Their collaborative skills are well-honed, and the result is an honest form of architecture – materials, texture, colour, form and light interact in sometimes surprising ways, but always in a genuine manner, with a clarity of purpose.
The members of the firm have seasoned experience with many of the challenges facing architects in the New York area. Abelow Sherman utilise their knowledge to lead a process that is as methodical as is possible, and that delivers to each client their best efforts. Precision, creativity, and technical expertise are always committed, and the solutions tailored to the particular project type and budget.

Alessandro Marchelli

Add: 15, Via Gozzellini, 14049 Nizza Monferrato, Asti, Italy
Tel: +39.0141.725135; Fax: +39.0141.703821
Web: www.alessandromarchelli.it

Alessandro Marchelli, chief designer, was born in Nizza Monferrato (Asti - Italy) on December 10th, 1964. As an interior and industrial designer, art director, consultant in public and private fields, he specialised in brand vision, management, concept design, design development, and so on.
From 1990, he has been founder and director of the design company Alessandro Marchelli + Designers (AM+D) who is an international and multicultural company, focusing on sensory interior architectures, and creative and experimental designs.

Alexa Nice Interior Design

Tel: +61408144083
Web: www.alexanice.com

Alexa Nice is founder and director of Alexa Nice Interior Design, specialising in high-end hospitality design. Nice is an extremely passionate and highly talented designer with her unique style and attention to detail often described as intricately creative and divinely opulent. With a formal qualification in Bachelor of Built Environment majoring in interior design, Alexa has an impressive portfolio that spans hospitality, commercial, retail and high-end residential, and has worked closely with one other creative director from the film industry on various prestigious interiors in Brisbane, Australia.

Apostrophy's The Synthesis Server

Add: 21/66 RCA block C Rama9 Rd. Bangkapi Huai kwang Bangkok 10310, Thailand
Tel : +66 87 360-3838; Fax : +66 2 664-6057
Web: www.apostrophys.com

Apostrophy's The Synthesis Server is run buy a group of designers from different backgrounds, directed by Pantavit Lawaroungchok. Apostrophy's the Synthesis Server was founded nine years ago during their time of studying architecture and established as a company in 2008. It started from a group of friends wanting to experimen their design knowledge from school to make their own design products, and learn how to make designs in other different areas by exchanging knowledge among themselves and others. Apostrophy's has been a new media design office offering a mixture of different design channels such as visual design (graphics, motion graphics, animation), game application, lighting programming design, media technology, installation art feature, interior and architecture.
The mission of the company is to use different arts and technology knowledge as tools to bring people to play in the spaces enabling them to participate in creating them by themselves through interactive games, exhibitions, motion graphics, etc. Their motto is 'We are not just designers but we're trying to make everybody designers…"

Architects EAT

Add: Level 2, 227 Commercial Road South Yarra, 3141 Victoria, Australia
Tel: 61 3 9824 0813; Fax: 61 3 9824 0843
Web: www.eatas.com.au

Architects EAT is a well-recognised creative firm for architecture and interior design. Established in 2000, the practice has collected numerous national awards, including the recent Australian Institute of Architects Victoria Awards 2010 for residential houses, the 2008 Interior Design Awards Best of State Awards for Commercial Interior and the 2007 Belle Apartment of the Year Award.
During the past ten years, their practice has deliberately maintained a policy of diversity, with clients from many sectors including private homes, high-rise residential developments, retail, local government and hospitality projects. Their work is based upon a solid foundation of design excellence, budget and programme control, proficient project management and the achievement of best value and architectural quality. Architects EAT is a practice driven by a consistent philosophical approach, not a predetermined style. As a result, they aim to create specifically detailed buildings that are intimately connected to the function and the context.

AS Scenario interiørarkitekter MNIL

Add: Pilestredet 75C, 0175 Oslo, Norway
Tel: 0047 22 93 12 50, E-mail: Info@scenario.no
Web: www.scenario.no

Their ambition is to visualise their clients´ profile, vision and personality through interior design. AS Scenario is an interior design practice with emphasis on professional planning, refurbishment, furnishings of commercial buildings and hotels, private housing and furniture design. Established in 1985 by Interior designer Linda Steen. Today, the office holds 26 interior designers, furniture designers, and administration with broad experience from different projects and education from both Norway and overseas.

Atelier Markgraph

Add: Atelier Markgraph GmbH, Ludwig-Landmann-Straße 349, D-60487 Frankfurt am Main, Germany
Tel: +49 (0) 69 97993-0, Fax: +49 (0) 69 97993-1181
Web: www.markgraph.de

Atelier Markgraph is a Frankfurt-based agency that has won many awards for spatial communication. The interdisciplinary design agency creates direct, three-dimensional experiences of brands and topics for exhibitions, museums, showrooms, trade shows and presentations. Clients include Mercedes-Benz, Deutsche Telekom, cities and museums.

Atelier Nini Andrade Silva

Add: Rua do Barão, nº 25 e 29,1100-072 Lisboa, Portugal
Tel: +351 21 812 3790
Web: www.niniandradesilva.com

Nini Andrade Silva Atelier is a brand of international reference in design, furniture design and interior architecture consultancy on a high level of quality and associated to an excellent hospitality service. Their company is directed by the renowned designer Nini Andrade Silva who has become a reference in the world of interior architecture and design, winning awards several times. Their team made up of architects, designers and decorators, is currently engaged in several projects worldwide, related with hotels, private habitations, restaurants and offices. In the near future, Nini Andrade Silva will expand her business map across Europe, North and South America, Asia, the Middle East and Africa. The Fontana Park Hotel and the The Vine Hotel projects were recently awarded at the European Hotel Design Awards. Nini Andrade Silva's success has been proudly reported in numerous and prestigious international newspapers and magazines. She was also mentioned several times in Andrew Martin's Yearbook – featuring 'World Leading Designers'.

Axis Mundi

Add: Axis Mundi Design LLC. 315 West 39th Street, suite 805 New York, NY 10018, USA
Tel: 212-643-2608
Web: www.axismundi.com

In a world increasingly dominated by the homogeneity of globalisation, they create meaningful designs with a cultural specificity. Recent projects have been featured in Metropolitan Home, Spaces, C3, Archiworld, and The New York Times, as well as on blogs such as Dezeen, Designboom, Domus, Inhabitat, ArchDaily, The Architect's Newspaper, Curbed, and BLDGBLOG. Axis Mundi's principal, John Beckmann received a grant from the Graham Foundation for Advanced Studies in the Fine Arts for the book The Virtual Dimension: Architecture, Representation and Crash Culture, Princeton Architectural Press, 1998. He is a graduate of Parsons School of Design.

Bluarch Architecture + Interiors

Add: 118 West 27th Street – Floor 11 - New York, New York 10001
Tel: 212 929 5989; Fax: 212 656 1626
Web: www.bluarch.com

bluarch architecture + interiors is an award-winning firm founded by Antonio Di Oronzo. It is a practice dedicated to design innovation and technical excellence providing complete services in master planning, architecture and interior design. At bluarch, architecture is an aesthetic and logical endeavour that offers shelter to layered human needs. It is a narrative of complex systems which offer beauty and efficiency through tension and decoration.
The growing intersection of the arts, science and technology is seen as the opportunity to research and represent human organic interaction. Digital tools and technologies are an integral part of the planning process and a preferred means to implement new approaches to design.
Based in New York City, the firm is recognised for both built and speculative work in both publications and exhibitions around the world. Its work has been exhibited at the MoMa, Life of the City (2002); The Van Alen Institute (New York City, 2005); Centro Arquitectum (Caracas - Venezuela, 2005), and published in books and magazines across the globe.

Bozhinovskidesign Studio

Add: Varna,Bulgaria
Tel: +359 898 245 334
Web: www.bozhinovskidesign.com

Located in Varna, Bulgaria, Bozhinovskidesign Studio has been in the field of interior design for four years. Innovative design and smart solutions are the driving principles in their projects. They offer a vision beyond imagination, showing the future through the lenses of the client's concepts and ideas.

BRC Imagination Arts

Add: 2711 Winona Ave, Burbank, CA, USA
Tel: (818) 841-8084
Web: http://brcweb.com

Since Bob Rogers founded the company in 1981, BRC has been entrusted with creating immersive experiences for some of the world's most respected brands. A few of these include Universal Studios, NASA, The Walt Disney Company, The Empire State Building, Korean Airlines, Dentsu, Tatweer, General Motors, Ford, Heineken, China Mobile, China Telecom, Volkswagen, and even entire countries participating in multiple world expo pavilions, including two for the United States of America.
Today's consumer demands to be wowed. They are savvy to traditional overt methods and seek a personalised engagement with the brands they support. Combining storytelling and immersive technologies enables BRC to dimensionalise brands in ways that traditional advertising simply cannot. By creating a compelling mythology and giving the visitor a role in the story, BRC creates brand experiences that forge powerful and lasting emotional connections to the brand–turning the casual consumer into a lifelong member of a tribe.

Büro Ueberholz

Add: Warndtstraße 7, 42285 Wuppertal, Germany
Tel: 02 02 280 96 -0, Fax: 02 02 280 96-66
Web: www.ueberholz.de

In dialogue with the customer, they design and realise places for encounters, with the aim of starting up and supporting processes of communication. They provide full service in the following areas of activity: fair construction, events service, shop construction, and exhibition and music architecture. With a team of architects and designers, they develop every fair booth from the first draft to construction.
In addition to contemporary fair architecture, oriented towards the corporate identity of the company, they also develop unusual presentation solutions, lighting concepts and detail solutions. With partners from catering, PR and communication design, they put together an all-inclusive worry-free package for their customers.

BWM Architekten und Partner

Add: Margaretenplatz 4/L1, A-1050 Vienna, Austria
Tel: +43 1 205 90 70; Fax: +43 1 205 90 70-20
Email: office@bwm.at
Web: www.bwm.at

Erich Bernard, Daniela Walten and Johann Moser are working together since 1998/99. In 2004 they founded BWM Architekten und Partner, a studio for architecture, planning and design based in Vienna. Markus Kaplan became junior partner in 2008.
Their main competencies include retail and corporate architecture, cultural projects and projects in public spaces, as well as structural engineering and urban development.

Casson Mann

Add: Casson Mann Designers, 45 Mitchell Street, London EC1V 3QD
Tel: 020 7324 1964, Fax: 020 7251 6238
Web: www.cassonmann.co.uk

Casson Mann is a team of designers dedicated to the delivery of innovative projects for their clients. The majority of these are museums and exhibitions, many of which have won awards.
They create responses to all types of projects and are sufficiently flexible to be able to design galleries, whole museums, temporary and travelling exhibitions, master planning and interpretative strategies.
In addition to museums and exhibitions, they have designed offices, listed building refurbishments, cafes, restaurants and hotels. They frequently head up large teams, always mindful of their responsibility to maintain quality and adhesion to the vision.
They have worked with most of the major national museums in the UK and have created some benchmark galleries including the British Galleries at the Victoria and Albert Museum, the Wellcome Wing Galleries at the Science Museum and the Churchill Museum at the Imperial War Museum, all located in London.

CL3 Architects Ltd.

Add: 15/F, Hong Kong Arts Centre, 2 Harbour Road, Hong Kong
Tel: 852 2527-1931; Fax: 852 2529-8392
Web: www.cl3.com

CL3 Architects Ltd. (CL3) is an innovative architecture and interior design studio in Asia, creating architectural and interior projects in areas such as hotel, hospitality, restaurants, retail, corporate, and art installation design. They are Hong Kong based with a staff of 65 and regional offices in Beijing, Shanghai and Bangkok.
Their clients include Crown Hotel & Casino, Shangri-La Hotels Group, Marina Bay Sands Corp, Marco Polo Hotel Group, Royal Pacific Hotel, etc. One of CL3' s proudest achievements is to hav received the Design for Asia Award 2004 from the Hong Kong Design Centre. In 2004, the company received the Architecture Firm Award from the American Institute of Architects (Hong Kong Chapter), the highest honour awarded by the Chapter.
The company has also been honoured with numerous design awards from the American Institute of Architects Hong Kong Chapter, the American Institute of Architects Northwest and Pacific Region, the Hong Kong Institute of Architects, the Hong Kong Design Association, the Hong Kong Design Centre (Design for Asia Award), the International Interior Design Magazine for the Best of the Year Award, and the International Hotel/Motel Restaurant show (IH/M&RS) for the Gold Key Award for excellence in hospitality design.

Concrete Architectural Associates

Add: Rozengracht 133 III, 1016 LV Amsterdam, the Netherlands
Tel: +31(0)20. 5200200; Fax: +31(0)20. 5200201
Web: www.concreteamsterdam.nl

Concrete consists of three companies: Concrete Architectural Associates, Concrete Reinforced and the scale model company Models+Monsters. Concrete's entire team consists of about 25 professional people.
Visual marketeers and interior designers, product designers and architects work on the projects in multidisciplinary teams. As a member of Concrete, founded in 1997, Concrete Architectural Associates is based in an old gym on Amsterdam's Rozengracht. Here, the designers work on total concepts in brainstorm sessions while Concrete develops total concepts for businesses and institutions.
The agency produces work which is commercially applicable. This involves creating total identities for a company, a building or an area. The work extends from interior design to urban development integration and from the building to its accessories. Concrete, for example, also sets the perimetres for the graphic work and considers how the client can present itself in the market.

Contzentrade® Designstudio

Add: Alicestrasse 7, 63456 Hanau, Germany
Tel: + 49 (0) 61 81 25 90 57, Fax: + 49 (0) 61 81 25 90 59
Email: mail@larscontzen.de
Web: http://www.larscontzen.com

Lars Contzen was born in 1970 Frankfurt, Main. After a background of many years in liberal fine arts, the focus of Lars Contzen shifted to the applied arts and the cutting edge between both disciplines. The emphasis of work of Contzentrade Designstudio deals with the surface of products, objects and spaces.
The idea is to build up a conceptional interplay about graphic or colour in the area of interior design. The Contzentrade Designstudio has 15 employees and digital production for wallpaper and background laminates.

D-HANDED

Add: 5F, No.126, Liuyizhonglu, Fuzhou, Fujian, China
Tel: 0591-88388882; Fax: 0591-88188856
Web: www.d-hand.cn

D-HANDED is a professional interior decorator design institution, which aims to create much perfect living conditions to their customers. The company, D-HANDED, has a highly effective practical design team, and they dedicate ourselves to offer high standard design service, especially in designing high-end homes, model rooms, office spaces, characteristic dining, and commercial offices.
A good design, they believe, should be done well in absorbing artistic and historical culture essences, taking every consideration of the customer's wishes. It is just the goal they pursue, which makes their design not only attain the customer's praise, but also good results repeatedly.

D'art Design Gruppe GmbH

Add: Haus am Pegel, Am Zollhafen 5,41460 Neuss, Germany
Tel: +49 (0)2131. 40 30 7 – 35, Fax: +49 (0)2131. 40 30 7 - 89
Web: www.d-art-design.de

The D'ART DESIGN GROUP is amongst the leading agencies for spatial communication in Germany and combines creative design qualities with interdisciplinary know-how. Having been rewarded with international design awards, the D'ART DESIGN GROUP creates brand and theme worlds for clients like Adidas, Arte, Audi, BZgA, E-Plus, Gabor, Gräfe und Unzer, Grundig, Lloyd, Panasonic, Philips, RWE and WMF.

David Kohn Architects

Add: 79 Stoneleigh Terrace London N19 5TZ
Tel:+44 0 20 7419 1817, Fax: +44 0 20 7209 0979
Web:www.davidkohn.co.uk

Winner of the Young Architect of the Year Award 2009, David Kohn Architects is a London based architectural practice founded by David Kohn in 2007. Recent projects include Flash, a temporary restaurant at the Royal Academy of Arts, which won a D&AD Yellow Pencil Award 2009, a house for Stuart Shave in Norfolk, a new art gallery for Modern Art, London and an urban design strategy for Deptford in partnership with Design for London.
In addition to practice, David is a writer on cultural issues, a design advisor to Newham Council and the Sorrell Foundation and a course leader at the London Metropolitan University. He studied architecture at the University of Cambridge and at Columbia University, New York, as a Fulbright Scholar.

Della Valle Bernheimer

Add: 20 Jay Street Suite 1003 Brooklyn, NY 11201, USA
Tel: 718 222 8155; Fax: 718 222 8157
Web: www.dbnyc.com

Founded in 1996 by Jared Della Valle and Andrew Bernheimer, Della Valle Bernheimer's portfolio includes affordable and high-end residential, commercial, hospitality, mixed-use, public architectural projects, furniture design, architectural design competitions, and art installations. DB is an award-winning and internationally-recognised design firm with a diverse range of projects across varied scales; they are forward-thinking, industrious, cost-attentive, and sustainable. The firm has been honoured on several occasions for cutting-edge design work, including citations from the New York City and New York State chapters of the AIA, amongst others.
DB was given an Honour Award from the New York City AIA for a sensitive intervention and restoration of Paul Rudolph's iconic home in Manhattan. In 2007, they were selected as an Emerging Voice by the Architectural League of New York, and were awarded 2010 Research and Development as well as Design Merit Awards from Architect Magazine and the AIA NYC Chapter.
The studio has a history of working in concert with complex consultant teams and believes that collaborative thinking yields critical and rigorous results. The opportunity to take a holistic approach to design, to understand the market, and to reinforce the image and perception is unique to DB.

Derlot Pty. Ltd.

Add: Unit3/15 Edmondstne St., West End, Queensland 4101, Australia
Tel: +61 (0)404682139
Web: www.derlot.com

Derlot Pty. Ltd. is a multidisciplinary studio focusing on projects that span product, furniture, branding, hotel design, interior design and art direction with clients both nationally and internationally. Their clients include IDEE-Sputnik of Japan, Planex of Australia, SIGG of Switzerland, COVO of Italy, Asahi of Japan, Mizuno of Japan UFL of New Zealand, Escofet of Spain, S&G of Australia, Nestle of Switzerland, the Queensland Art Gallery and the design of the first of the Design Hotels in Australia.
As the director of Derlot Pty. Ltd., Mr. Alexander Lotersztain was born in Buenos Aires, Argentina in 1977, and graduated from design at Griffith University QCA in 2000. He has participated in international exhibitions with Sputnik, Designers Block London, Tokyo, Milano, New York, San Francisco, Berlin, Moscow and some of his products as part of the design collection at the Pompidou Museum in Paris.
Mr. Lotersztain recently won the Inaugural Queensland Premier Smart State Designer of the Year Fellowship Award 2010. He was named among 100 of the most influential designers worldwide by Phaidon, the top ten most influential faces in design by Scene Design Quarterly 2007 and placed in top ten in 100 Young Brightest Australian Achievers Bayer/Bulletin Award. Has won many awards in both product and interior design and his work has appeared in design journals around the world. Alexander is also part of the Smart State Design Council for the Queensland Government in Australia, drafting the Smart State design Strategy for 2020.

Design Spirits Co., Ltd.

Add: 2-18-2-202 Ohara setagaya tokyo 156-0041, Japan
Tel: +81 3 3324 9901
Web: www.design-spirits.com

Born in Tokyo Japan in 1967, chief interior designer Yukichi Kawai established Design Spirits Co. Ltd in 2003. With the spirit of craftsmanship and earnestness, Design Spirits believes that "An essence makes a space. They quest for that essence, to create a space with long life. As craftsman, this is their design spirits."

DesignLSM

Add: designLSM BrightonThe Bath House, 58 Livingstone Road, Hove, East Sussex, BN3 3WL, UK
Tel: 01273 820033, Fax: 01273 820058
Web: www.designlsm.com

DesignLSM, based in Hove East Sussex, is an integrated design practice comprising of interior designers, graphic design and architects. They have been creating award-winning design for their clients for over two decades and continue to work with some of the leading operators within the leisure industry. Their diverse portfolio includes independent and national hotels, high street restaurants and bar chains, independent restaurateurs, food retail, fashion retail, clubs, casinos and commercial and residential developments.

Dimitris Naoumis Architect Studies Office

Add: 24 Psychari str, Athens, Greece
Tel:+30 210 2233 434
Web:www.naoumis.com

Dimitris Naoumis has studied interior design, product design and industrial design. He has also worked as a professor of architectural design for six years. His office is located in Athens, Greece. For the last 13 years, his Architect Studies office has been responsible for designing many professional office spaces, house interiors, clubs, restaurants, and etc. Dimitris Naoumis has also created many product design objects. Many of his projects have been featured in local and international publications. Dimitris Naoumis Architect Studies Office takes care of all the designs and constructing processes in each project until final completion.

Erges Architecture & Design

Add: Sporta 2a - 418, Riga, Latvia
Tel / Fax: +371 67334093,
Web: http://www.erges.com

For years, Erges Architecture & Design has been working in field of interior design. Their motto is "Design is not just what we see, but also what we feel..." They aim to create aesthetically refined and exclusive interiors that induce strong feelings and satisfaction even from the most demanding customers. Every project is a special story they approach very tremulously, so all their projects are handled at a highly technical and artistic level.

Estilo Arquitectura

Add: Calle 39 Num. 490 por 54 y 56 Col. Centro, Merida, Yucatan, Mexico C.P.97000, Mexico
Tel: 999 927 39 03
Web: www.estiloyucatan.com

Estilo Arquitectura is a new architecture studio established on 2004 in the city of Merida. The studio was formed by a group of architects united by a common philosophy: to create spaces for the 21st century. The spaces are either new and original creations, or the product of reinterpreting established structures through a new approach. They believe in architecture as an art-science fusion that is used to create habitats and not only monuments.
They work inside a Latin-American context and they believe in using local economic and material resources not as a fashion statement or a passing fad but for their convenience of use and their inherent beauty.
They believe that each one of the rough materials they use contains its own unique quality and it is the job and objective of the architect to extract a refined version of this quality and display it as an integral and essential part of the finished product.
They create an architecture that is emotionally charged and not sensationalised, they want the public to live and experience an architecture that it is not only visual but that is also an architecture that stimulates the five senses; they want people to breathe, see, smell and taste their architecture.

Front Studio

Add: 187 Lafayette St, Fl 6 New York, Ny 10013, USA
Tel: (212) 334-6820; Fax: (212) 334-6822
Web: www.frontstudio.com

Founded in 2001, the enterprising firm of Front Studio is noted for its ability to blur the distinctions between art and architecture. The practice has won several international competitions which challenge conventional notions of space, often through the evocation of visionary ideas. Under the stewardship of Yen Ha and Michi Yanagishita, Front Studio pursues a thoughtful and creative approach to design.
Reluctant to participate in current trends and fashions, Front Studio's commitment to creativity ensures that every project undergoes a careful and comprehensive investigation. In addition to rigorous design methods, the firm instills projects with a sense of humour, recognisable in their whimsical proposals.
Front Studio always transcends client expectations by offering unique solutions to complement programmatic requirements. Fluent in French, Vietnamese and Japanese, Michi and Yen work on an international scale, collaborating with foreign clients based locally and abroad. Whether speculative or realised, Front Studio is constantly inspired by its surroundings, discovering innovation and imagination in every opportunity.

Global Architectural Development

Add: Tesvikiye Cad, 3B Gunes Apt, Tesvikiye Istanbul 34367, Turkey
Tel: +90 212 327 5125; Fax: +90 212 258 1663
Web: gadarchitecture.com

Global Architectural Development is an Istanbul and New York based company, which performs architectural practice, research and concept design since 1994 and whose partners are Gokhan Avcioglu and Ozlem Ercil Avcioglu, with their global collaborators. Contemporary and current architecture, urbanism, software, consumer habits and behaviours and approaching the projects holistically are among its field of interests. GAD understands architecture as a practice that relies on the experiment, values historical precedents and new ways to combine both in a mutually benefiting fashion.
GAD Architecture is committed to finding innovative approaches to architecture and creating new spatial experiences with projects and ideas. GAD has won numerous awards including the 1997 Turkish Architecture Prize for the design of a public park in Istanbul and the 2001 Cimsa Design Prize for outdoor seating, a bronze medal in Miami Biennale for Borusan Exhibition Centre in 2003. The public park in 1998 and in 2004, while the Esma Sultan Venue in 2001 was short listed for Aga Khan Award for Architecture. GAD has offices in Istanbul, New York and Bodrum.

GCA Arquitectos Asociados

Add: Valencia, 289 - 08009 Barcelona
Tel: +34 934 761 800
Web: http://www.gcaarq.com

GCA Arquitectos Asociados was founded in 1986 by Josep Juanpere and Antonio Puig. GCA projects architecture, urbanism and interior design with a multidisciplinary group of professionals. GCA offers a wide range of services to cover all of their clients' needs, from establishing the first idea, through the development of Design and Construction to the completion of the work and assitance of the initial users, all including the management of the required permits. GCA projects and develops architecture, urbanism and interior design, both for public and private sectors.
The typologies of the projects are: office buildings, hotels, housing, single family houses, commercial centers, academic and civic buildings and marine design.

Giancarlo Zema Design Group

Add: Via della Giuliana 32, 00195 Rome, Italy
Tel: +39 06 372 47 72; Fax: +39 06 375 00 625
Web: www. giancarlozema.com

The Giancarlo Zema Design Group is an architecture studio in Rome, specialised in semi-submerged architectural structures, marine parks, floating habitats and yacht design. It was founded in 2001 by the architect Giancarlo Zema as a dynamic and flexible organisation, which guarantees the whole design process, from the concept to the executive details.
Their projects are frequently shown in European exhibitions and published in the most important scientific, design, nautical and architecture magazines. They believe that the future of architecture is on the water and that shortly humanity will be more and more inclined towards living in semi-submerged environments.
For this reason, their efforts are geared towards creating innovative architecture in harmony with nature. With this aim in mind, they have become partners with ZLH (Pty) Ltd, a consulting engineers company in South Africa for the engineering of their projects.

Greg Natale Design

Add: Studio 6 Level 3, 35 Buckingham Street, Surry Hills NSW 2010, Australia
Tel: 61 (0)2 8399 2103; Fax: 61 (0)2 8399 3104

Established in 2001 and based in Sydney, Greg Natale Design is an award-winning firm of highly skilled architects and interior designers that has become recognised as one of the most innovative emerging design practices in the country.
Greg Natale Design provides a fully integrated, personalised service that ensures quality, creativity and, above all, client satisfaction. Central to the company practice is a unique sense of style that reflects an attention to detail and design excellence, whether residential, hospitality, retail, corporate or product design.
With many projects featured in national and international design magazines and books, Greg Natale Design's work has been described as bold, exciting, dynamic, glamorous, sophisticated, "having attitude" and "verging on kitsch". Greg Natale Design has also won or been shortlisted for a number of prestigious awards from all over the world.

HSD Design

Add: E-16, E-17 Oriental Garden Huaqiao City, Nanshan District, Shenzhen, China
Tel: 0755-82879961; Fax: 0755-26908587
Web: www.h-sd.cn

HSD is a young talented international design team who focuses on contemporary design. It becomes the forerunner of architectural design, interior design and landscape design because of the innovative design throughout its works. HSD explores potential possibilities beyond traditional function and makes every single design special and vivid. HSD utilises the advanced digital tool and design methodology to create contemporary Chinese design. HSD believes that the origin of design is function. A successful design is based on the successful corporation between designer and client. The association of HSD and the consultants from the US and Canada will provide the highest service for its clients.

II BY IV Design Associates

Add: 77 Mowat Avenue, Suite 109, Toronto M6K 3E3, Canada
Tel: 416 531 2224; Fax: 416 642 0102
Web: www.iibyiv.com

Based out of Toronto Canada, II BY IV Design Associates have been in operation for 20 years. They are a boutique firm of 19 very talented and passionate people. Internationally, II BY IV has been honoured with more than 200 awards for interior design, lighting design, and the design of furniture and furnishings, in restaurant, retail, condominium, hotel, nightclub, exhibits, showroom, and office projects. The firm has been declared one of the world's Top 50 Retail Designers. Their work has been featured in several TV productions and in countless publications from around the world. The firm's work demonstrates an expert interpretation of current and emerging consumer lifestyles, attitudes, and expectations, applied to the design of residential, retail, hospitality, commercial and special-purpose interiors.

Ilaria Marelli Studio

Add: Via Mentana, 12, 22100 Como, Italy
Tel: +39 031 2491906; Fax: +39 031 2759859
Web: www.ilariamarelli.com

Ilaria Marelli, architect and designer, founded the creative lab Ilaria Marelli Studio in 2004, specialising in product, exhibition and interior design. The design studio also provides strategy and trend consultancy to fashion and design companies. Ilaria Marelli was designated by the Italian Culture Ministry to be member of the first Italian Design Council, and she is promoting the first Italian project of co-housing. In 2008, Ilaria Marelli received MILANODONNA Award 2008, in the Giovani Donne (young women) category, founded and assigned by Milan mayor Letizia Moratti.

Indyk Architects

Add: 4a Begg lane Paddington NSW, Sydney, Australia
Tel: 93616850; Fax: 93607953
Web: www.indykarchitects.com.au

Indyk Architects is a small personal office which collectively aims for innovation in design. Re-configured in 1998 upon Shelley Indyk's return from three years overseas, the practice works out of Begg Lane Studio in Paddington.
The Studio is a base for a collection of individuals with unique skills under one roof. They actively seek to collaborate, building up networks which incorporate specific areas of expertise appropriate to each given project. Indyk herself has a great love of landscape; of cultural diversity; and of the genius loci of place. She is often involved in projects that demand an openness and understanding of cooperation.

INTERNO B

Location: Rome, Italy
Tel: +39 3386026208
Email: info@internob.com; internob@alice.it
Website: www.internob.com

INTERNO B is specialised in the interior design and craftsmanship of furnitures. Created by Barbara Buzi, an artist before a designer, INTERNO B is the result of a strong passion for applied creativity. Within the ART-Lab, a real artistic laboratory, furnishing elements arise from a combination of ideas, techniques and materials of various kinds, often reused, wisely following the tradition of craftsmanship. The main objective is to design unique environments far from common standards and make them absolutely individual.

Iodice Architetti

Add: palazzo fiorentino via guglielmo santelice 52 81031 aversa(ce)
Tel:+39 081 8130100 Fax: +39 081 8130100
Web: http://www.iodicearchitetti.it

The study Iodice Architetti works on national and international projects and competitions for a long time. The scopes of planning span urban architecture to interior design.
Their engagement is to combine an experimental dimension with a professional completeness so as to respond to complex design programmes of every scale, using an established network of expert advisory (structures, installations, cost control, environmental impact).
The transformation of the space touches various aspects, the project is only one of these; this oscillates between numerous solicitations that are only apparently conflicted. In opposition to the ultimate tendencies, the group pays great attention to be the relation between shape and content, good architecture cannot be separated by a conscious fusion of these two aspects.
The dimension of the real and technological innovation are flanked constantly at a conceptual process, convinced that every project necessitates a good idea at the beginning. They think that architecture, as is literature, music or painting, is an essential part of culture, of every culture in every time.

Janson Goldstein

Add: 180 VARICK STREET SUITE 1414 NEW YORK, NY 10014
Tel: 212.691.1611 x10; Fax: 212.691.2244
Web: www.jansongoldstein.com

Janson Goldstein is a full service architecture and interior design firm that creates environments for a wide range of retail, residential and commercial clients in the US and abroad. Founded by architects Mark Janson and Hal Goldstein in 1995, and joined by retail specialist Steven Scuro in 2000, Janson Goldstein specialises in developing solutions particular to the challenges of each project. The firm operates on the assumption that design is only the beginning, and devotes its considerable talents to ensuring that projects are properly phased and coordinated with respect to schedule and budget.
Janson Goldstein's retail practice focuses on providing responses to image and merchandising issues, while working to establish and reinforce a unique presence for each client. The firm's roster of retailers includes many fashion industry leaders, such as Giorgio Armani, Salvatore Ferragamo, Burberry, Donna Karan, Calvin Klein, Saks Fifth Avenue, and Holt Renfrew. Janson Goldstein's work encompasses commercial and hospitality design as well.
Janson Goldstein's modernism is clearly demonstrated in its high-end residential projects, which occupy some of Manhattan's most enviable addresses. The contrast of project types illustrates the firm's philosophy that a diversity of challenges and responses enriches the design process and the development of each unique undertaking. Each Janson Goldstein project reveals the firm's approach to smart space planning, refined materials, sophisticated colour palettes, and a mix of classic and custom furnishings.

Joey Ho Design Ltd

Add: Unit 1601-1602 16/F Car Po Commercial Building, 18-20 Lyndhurst Terrace Central, Hong Kong
Tel: 852 2850 8732; Fax: 852 2850 8972
Web: www.joeyhodesign.com

Joey Ho graduated from The University of Hong Kong (Master of Architecture) and National University of Singapore (Bachelor of Architectural Study). Joey eventually chose Hong Kong as the base for his architectural design firm Joey Ho Design Limited and set up Basheer Design Books (Hong Kong) Ltd.
Over the past years, Joey has won over 70 awards and has established a high profile client list in the hospitality, residential, institutional and retail sectors with projects spread over different cities including Hong Kong, Singapore and the Greater China region.

Jonas Wagell Design & Architecture

Add: Timmermansgatan 5 SE-118 25 Stockholm, Sweden
Tel: +46 8 40390322
Web: www.jonaswagell.se

Jonas Wagell is a Swedish architect and designer with a back record in strategic project management and marketing. In 2008, he was named one of the world's 50 hottest young architects by Wallpaper* magazine and introduced the awarded prefab house concept Mini House. In 2009, Wagell founded the design brand Hello Industry which first collection was announced as Best of Stockholm Design Week 2009 by Wallpaper*. During 2010 the studio is designing new products for Muuto, Normann Copenhagen, Mitab, Bergaform and more, but is also approaching architecture projects such as bars, hotels and museums.

Kauffmann Theilig & Partner

Add: Kauffmann Theilig & Partner, Freie Architekten BDA, Zeppelinstraße 10, D-73760 Ostfildern, Gemany
Tel: +49 (0) 711 45122 -0, Fax: +49 (0) 711 45122 -40
Web: www.ktp-architekten.de

Kauffmann Theilig & Partner is an architectural office near Stuttgart which was established in 1988 by Prof. Andreas Theilig and Dieter Ben Kauffmann. Later on Rainer Lenz and Manfred Ehrle became partners. The office is involved in planning and realising various sized projects in the whole field of building construction as well as exhibition design and big sized projects and concepts in china. The office has cultivated an intensive collaboration with experts and engineers from different specialties to gain integral architectural solutions within interdisciplinary teams. The innovative work of KTP has been awarded with different architecture and design prizes worldwide.

Kengo Kuma & Associates

Add: 2-24-8 Minami Aoyama, Minato-ku, Tokyo 107.0062, Japan
Tel: +81.3.3401.7721; Fax+81.3.3401.7778
Web: www.kkaa.co.jp

Kengo Kuma was born in Kanagawa, Japan in 1954. He completed his master's degree at the University of Tokyo in 1979. From 1985 to 1986, he studied at Columbia University as Visiting Scholar. He established Kengo Kuma & Associates in 1990 in Aoyama, Tokyo. From 2001 to 2008, he taught at the Faculty of Science and Technology at Keio University. In 2009 he was installed as professor of the University of Tokyo.
Among Kuma's major works are the Kirosan Observatory (1995), Water/Glass (1995, for which he received the AIA Benedictus Award), Venice Biennale/Space Design of Japanese Pavilion (1995), Stage in Forest, Toyoma Center for Performance Arts (1997, for which he received the 1997 Architectural Institute of Japan Annual Award), Stone Museum (2000, for which he received International Stone Architecture Award 2001), Bato-machi Hiroshige Museum (2001, for which he received The Murano Prize). A number of large scale projects are now going on in Europe and China. He was awarded the International Spirit of Nature Wood Architecture Award in 2002 (Finland), International Architecture Awards for the Best New Global Design for Chokkura Plaza and Shelter in 2007, and Energy Performance + Architecture Award in 2008 (France).

Kit Kemp

Add: 79 Crosby Street, New York, NY, United States, 10012, USA
Tel: +1 212 226 6400; Fax: +1 212 226 0055
Web: crosbystreethotel.com

Kit Kemp, with her husband Tim, owns the exclusive townhouse hotel group Firmdale Hotels. Firmdale comprises seven luxury boutique hotels: Covent Garden Hotel, Charlotte Street Hotel, Number Sixteen, Knightsbridge Hotel, The Soho Hotel, Haymarket Hotel in London and the Crosby Street Hotel in New York. Each attracts discerning international guests from the world of media, entertainment, fashion and the arts.
Kit Kemp, as design director has been responsible for the interiors of all properties. Firmdale is innovative in its field. It has acquired dilapidated properties such as warehouses, hospitals and car parks and has created from them small five star hotels which are internationally respected. In so doing, Firmdale has injected new energy and life into neglected areas.
For example, The Soho Hotel was originally a run down NCP car park. By creating the hotel with its new lighting, pavements and works of art, the immediate area has been transformed, and been given new life. Kit Kemp has received many awards over the years. These include the Andrew Martin International Interior Designer of the Year Award (2008), British House & Garden magazine's Hotel Designer of the Year (2008) and the The Crown Estate's Urban Business Award (2007). Other awards include Wallpaper magazine's Best Suite in the World and Tatler magazine's Most Glamorous Hotel in the World.

Koko Architecture

Add: 448 w 16th st, 5th floor ste 7 ny, ny 10011
Tel: 212+206+3638; Fax:212+206+3654
Web: www.kokoarch.com

Koko Architecture is a creative partnership established by the husband and wife team of Adam Weintraub and Mishi Hosono. The Studio, founded in 2000, gives them the opportunity to formally combine their diverse backgrounds and extensive experience in a multidisciplinary design forum. While centered on architecture, the Koko studio also encompasses city planning, architecture, and interior design. The Studio was named as one of ten "faces of the future" by the American Institute of Architects, New York Chapter. A film presenting recent projects by Koko was presented in the New York Center for Architecture. Koko's Projects have been featured in various publications including The New York Times, Cookie Magazine, Contract Magazine, Oculus, and Metropolis.

Koncept Stockholm AB

Add: Grev Turegatan 29, 114 28 Stockholm, Sweden
Tel: +46 (0)8-54587900, Fax +46 (0)8-54587920
Web: www.koncept.se

Koncept Stockholm AB is a unique office with clients and commissions from all over the world. The office is based in Stockholm where 34 employees work with design, architecture and concept development. Their clients can be found in the hotels, retail and Office sectors. Koncept designs unique environments which create value and a competitive advantage for their clients.

LAVA

Add: Laboratory for Visionary Architecture Asia Pacific, 72 Campbell, Street Surry Hills Sydney NSW 2010, Australia
Tel: 61 2 92801475; Fax: 61 2 92818125
Web: www.l-a-v-a.net

LAVA combines digital workflow, contemporary materials and the latest digital fabrication technologies with the aim of achieving more with less: more architecture with less material/energy/time/cost. LAVA is directed by Chris Bosse, Alexander Rieck and Tobias Wallisser with offices in Sydney and Stuttgart. Projects include the centre of Masdar, the world's first eco city in the UAE, Michael Schumacher Tower UAE, Future Hotel Showcase Germany, architectural installations such as Green Void, Digital Origami, Origami Tigers and Tower Skin which was winner of the ZEROprize Re-Skinning Awards.

Lee Broom

Add: Lee Broom, Electra House, 93 Rivington Street,
London, EC2A 3AY, UK
Tel: 020 7820 0742
Web: www.leebroom.com

Lee Broom founded his company eight years ago and has since gone on to become one of the UK's leading interior and product designers. In his career to date, Broom has designed over 35 bars and restaurant venues in London and the UK and has won 15 industry awards including Time Out's Best Bar award for Lost Society in Battersea. In 2007, he launched his first furniture collection Neo Neon to critical acclaim and has launched a new collection each year ever since, mapping countries such as London, Paris, New York, Hong Kong and The Middle East.
Broom's work has been featured in most major broadsheet and interior design publications, The Times has dubbed Broom as "the pin up boy of British manufacturing".

Lin Kaixin

Add: Room# 1003, 16F, Hongyuan Skycity B, 246# Hualin Road,
Fuzhou, China
Tel.: 0591-87404886

Chinese interior architect Lin kaixin founded Linkaixin Design, a professional interior design company, in April, 2005. Linkaixin Design has an excellent design team who create high-quality design projects all over the country, focusing on offering high standard design service including real estate business, financial business, hospitality industry, and private club.
Linkaixin Design dedicate themselves to academic communication, actively paticipate in interior design meetings and design competitions both at home and abroad. Many projects were published in professional magazines and books.

LISPACE

Add: E201, No.46 Fangjiahutong, Dongcheng District,
100007 Beijing, China
Tel: (86)10 87747807; Fax: (86)10 58859293
Web: www.lispace.com.cn

As a new generation specialist interior design group, LISPACE's design services focus on architecture, interior, furniture and decoration art. Their goal is to create special environments that lift the spirit, seek the perfect unity of spirit and function. Their works cover a wide range including hotel, club, restaurant, office, commercial space, residential space and exhibition, etc. LISPACE has office in Beijing and London.
As the creative director of Lispace, Jia Li has 10 years of experience In exterior and interior design. He seeks perfect uniform of spirit and function. His design emphasises on space and on the understanding between social form and culture.
His works involve architecture, interior, visual communication, furniture and home accessories. In the last three years, Jiali's works focus on boutique shops, sales centres (one has been awarded Golden Prize of 2008 at the China International Interior Design Biennial), office buildings (one has been awarded 2008 Asia Pacific Interior Design Award) and hotel design (one has been nominated for the 2008 Best Hotel Design, and one has received First Prize of the 2007 China Hotel Design Awards).

Logica: architettura

Add: 20, via Giasone del Maino, 20146 Milano, Italy
Tel: +39 02 4390815 F ax:+39 0243983877
Web: www.logica-architettura.it

Logica: architettura (founded in 1998 by Riccardo Salvi) primarily deals with interior, furniture and industrial design from the stage of analysis and to conception, the drafting of preliminary details, final constructional design, to the supervision of realisation, time and cost control, consignment to the client of the finished work and Logica: architettura defines a complete set of services that usually consists of: analysis of technical-economic feasibility, structural design, thermo technical and electrical services design, health and safety and firefighting control, management of execution supported by planning activity.
This approach ensures, since the conception phase, the optimisation of the project for functionality, economy and observance of time of accomplishment. Dedicated to research, they continually look for new techniques of construction, new materials, innovative technologies and always conceptualising design philosophies.

Luchetti Krelle Pty Ltd.

Add: 56 Cooper Street Surry Hills NSW 2010, Australia
Tel: 61 2 9699 3425
Web: http://luchettikrelle.com

Luchetti Krelle is an award-winning Surry Hills based, interior design firm established by partners Stuart Krelle and Rachel Luchetti. Although Luchetti Krelle maintains a diverse portfolio, its primary focus is in the hospitality sector.
As the various disciplines of design often overlap and integrate, Luchetti Krelle endeavours to offer a total concept; this includes branding and identity design, customised furniture and fitting design, salvaging and appropriation and even sourcing site locations. The result is unique and customised spaces that respond to client briefs and anticipate future trends whilst acknowledging current international design styles. Luchetti Krelle's focus on developing a strong relationship with the client, allowing for a collaborative and dynamic design process and the ability to offer a committed and personalised approach to each project. This designer-client relationship is fostered from conception to completion of projects through the various stages like concept design, documentation, tendering and project management processes.
Luchetti Krelle's success can be attributed to the company's commitment to extending itself beyond expectations to achieve a character and tone that fits perfectly with each design brief.

Maison Moschino

Add: Viale Monte Grappa, 12 20124 Milano (MI), Italy
Tel: 02 29 00 98 58, Fax: 02 63 79 38 65
Email: maisonmoschino@mobygest.it
Web: www.maisonmoschino.com

In 2010 Hotelphilosophy launches its first fashion hotel with the long-awaited opening of the Maison Moschino in Milan. The hotel – whose creativity is led by Rossella Jardini and Moschino's creative team – is located in the old neoclassical railway station on Viale Monte Grappa, 12, that opened in 1840 for the Milan-Monza route. Its design reflects Moschino's distinctive style, where the ordinary is brushed against with the surreal.

Marc & Chantal Design

Add: Room 401, 4/F, Arion Commercial Centre,
2-12 Queen's Road West, Hong Kong
Tel: +852 2543 7744; Fax: +852 2544 9170
Web: www.marc-chantal.com

Marc & Chantal Design was founded in Hong Kong in 1992 by Marc Brulhart, Marc Cansier and Chantal Rechaussat. The vision was to create a studio that would cross-over design disciplines and answer emerging needs in an holistic, rather than segmented approach. Today the company is fuelled by the talent and creativity of 30 individuals, harnessing this accumulated know-how in crafting unique multi-dimensional brand experiences.

The partners were guided by their design education in Paris and Milan to develop an open working environment, one in which lateral thinking and creative interaction are encouraged and nurtured. With 18 years of experience in connecting major international brands and corporations to the Asia Pacific market, the studio is now more than ever dedicated to act as a bridge between Eastern and Western cultures, and has recently started bringing its expertise and sensibility to major Chinese companies such as China Mobile and Yintai Property.

Marc Cansier and Chantal Rechaussat both studied fine arts and graphic design at the Ecole Superieure d'Art Graphique (Atelier Penninghen) in Paris. Marc Brulhart studied product and interior design at the European Institute of Design in Milan.

Marcel Wanders Studio

Add: P.O. Box 11332 1001 GH Amsterdam, the Netherlands
Tel: 31 (0)20 422 13 39; Fax: 31 (0)20 68 150 56
Web: www.marcelwanders.com

Marcel Wanders grew up in Boxtel, the Netherlands and graduated cum laude from the School of the Arts in Arnheim in 1988. Marcel Wanders' fame started with his iconic Knotted Chair, which he produced for Droog Design in 1996.

He is now ubiquitous, designing for the biggest European contemporary design manufacturers like B&B Italia, Bisazza, Poliform, Moroso, Flos, Boffi, Cappellini and Moooi of which he is also art director and co-owner.

Founded in 2000, Moooi has grown into an internationally renowned design label. Additionally, Marcel Wanders is involved in several design partnerships including Randstad, Bombay Sapphire, Mandarina Duck, Puma and Swarovski including consumer home appliances with Holland Electro.

Marshall Kusinski Design Consultants

Add: 803 Wellington Street, West Perth WA 6005, Australia
Tel: 08 9321 7955; Fax: 08 9321 7111
Web: www.mkdc.com.au

Founded in 1992 and based in Perth, Marshall Kusinski Design Consultants is an award winning practice of interior designers. Marshall Kusinski is one of the most respected design firms in Western Australia.

Company directors, Melanie Marshall and Kathleen Kusinski employ dynamic and experienced professionals working in a team based studio environment. Services include building analysis, brief development, programming, financial reports and budgets, space planning and design, detailed design documentation, liaison with council, co-ordination of sub consultants, tender management, contract administration, project management and safety management.

Marshall Kusinski are members of the Design Institute of Australia and the Green Building Council of Australia. Marshall Kusinski recognises that their success depends on understanding what makes a company unique. Working in collaboration, the long-term corporate goals of each client are implemented into flexible and functional solutions. Delivering projects on time and on budget, Marshall Kusinski value the experience of their team and other specialist fields, such as mechanical, electrical, communications and audio visual consultants, graphic designers, quantity surveyors and Feng Shui Masters.

Mass Studies

Add: Fuji Bldg 4F, 683-140 Hannam 2-dong Yongsan-gu,
Seoul 140-892, Korea
Tel: +82 (0)2 790 6528/9; Fax: +82 (0)2 790 6438
Web: www.massstudies.com

Mass Studies was founded in 2003 by Minsuk Cho in Seoul, Korea, as a critical investigation of architecture in the context of mass production, intensely over-populated urban conditions, and other emergent cultural niches that define contemporary society. Amid many frictions defining spatial conditions in the twenty-first century, namely past vs. future, local vs. global, utopia vs. reality, and individual vs. collective, Mass Studies focuses on the operative complexity of these multiple conditions instead of striving for a singular, unified perspective.

For each architectural project, which exists across a wide range of scales, Mass Studies explores issues such as spatial systems/matrices, building materials/techniques, and typological divergences to foster a vision that allows the discovery of new socio-cultural potential.

Minsuk Cho was born in Seoul and graduated from the Architectural Engineering Department of Yonsei University (Seoul, Korea) and the Graduate School of Architecture at Columbia University (New York). In 2003, he opened his own firm, Mass Studies. He has received many awards, including first prize in the 1994 Shinkenchiku International Residential Architecture Competition for new dwelling design, the Architectural League of New York's Young Architects Award in 2000 for his work at Cho Slade Architecture, and two U.S. Progressive Architecture Awards (Citations) for Von Erlach House in 1999 and Dalki Theme Park in 2003.

Matt Gibson A+D

Add: 29 Derby St Collingwood, victoria, Australia
Tel: +61 3 9419 6677; Fax +61 3 9419 6644
Web: www.mattgibson.com.au

Matt Gibson Architecture + Design Pty Ltd is a design based Melbourne practice that provides architectural, interior, landscape and furniture design services. The work of Matt Gibson Architecture + Design is based upon a solid foundation of design excellence, including budget and programme control, proficient project management and the achievement of best value and architectural quality.

Matt Gibson Architecture + Design is rapidly growing a reputation as one of Melbourne's best young architectural practices featuring regularly in local and international design publications. MG A+D's work has been included in exhibitions and is regularly short listed for awards.

The practice has won a number of awards including the national award for Best Emerging Practice in 2005 and national awards since for various categories for residential, corporate and retail projects. Most recently MG A+D won the 2009 World Award for Retail Design presented in Dubai for the experimental project, The Coop.

Matteo Thun & Partners

Add: Via Appiani 9 20121 Milano, Italy
Tel: +39 02 6556911, Fax +39 02 6570646
Web: http://www.matteothun.com

Matteo Thun was born in Bolzano, Italy, in 1952, studied at the Salzburg Academy under Oskar Kokoschka, took his degree in architecture in Florence in 1975 with Adolfo Natalini and moved to Milan in 1978, where he met and started working with Ettore Sottsass.

In 1981, he was a co-founder of the Memphis group, the design movement that so shaped events in the eighties. The next year, the Vienna Academy for Applied Arts appointed him to the chair in product design and ceramics. Leaving Memphis, he founded the Studio Matteo Thun in Milan in 1984 and served as Creative Director with Swatch in 1990-93.

Matteo Thun has won the ADI Compasso d'Oro Award for design excellence three times and only recently has received the Wallpaper* Design Awards 2010. His Side Hotel in Hamburg was chosen as Hotel of the Year in 2001, the Vigilius mountain resort won the Wallpaper* Design Award in 2004 and the Radisson SAS Frankfurt was chosen as the best hotel opened in the year for the Worldwide Hospitality Awards in 2005.

The Prix Acier Construction was given to him for the Hugo Boss Strategic Business Unit in Switzerland in 2007. Matteo Thun was inducted into the Interior Hall of Fame in New York in December 2004 and is a member of RIBA, the Royal Association of British Architects.

Max Bentheim

Add: 48 Amwell Street, London, EC1R 1XS, UK
Tel: +44(0)20 7278 3295
Web: www.maxbentheim.com

Max Bentheim is an exciting multidisciplinary design agency providing a variety of unique interiors and design solutions for the high-end residential market and five star hospitality industry.

They are a young, progressive team of highly professional, multi-faceted and dedicated designers, project managers and FF & E procurement specialists. Like other creative disciplines, they see their works as ever-changing. This allows them to be as streetwise, up-to-date and exciting as necessary to help their clients achieve their commercial goals and market recognition in their field.

They share no less than four languages between them to be able to undertake projects not only in the UK but wherever their international client bases his own properties. Avoiding a signature look, Max Bentheim interprets the client's style and individuality to create clean, defined interiors where quality materials and attention to detail are priorities. Their philosophy is one of individuality, holistic approach, strong client relationship and an underlying passion for design.

Max Bentheim has been nominated for the FX International Interior Design Awards 2010 in the category: Interior Design Practice of the Year 2010. They have also won the prestigious MIXOLOGY Environmental Design Award 2010. With further nomination at the 2010 European Hotel Design Awards in the categories Best New Build, Best Lobby & Public Areas, Best Spa & Wellness Area and Sustainability, Max Bentheim has deservedly received recognition for the continued success in producing innovative and inspiring interior designs for the hospitality industry.

Melanie Hall

Tel: +62 816 848 954
Web: www.luna2.com

MELANIE Hall is the owner and designer of Luna2 Inc. The Bali-based British entrepreneur has resided in Indonesia for 12 years; her vision for Luna2 private hotel was to create a brand new concept: a private hotel which would raise the benchmark in holiday-going by way of its prime location, its visionary design, its super-star service and unrivalled dining experience, all within the intimacy of a private home.

Melanie says of her design approach, "We revere the past, we welcome the future, and we like to have fun in the process!" Melanie is currently expanding the Luna2 brand regionally, and globally thereafter. Her new project, Luna2 studios, again unique as a studio hotel, is situated next to Luna2 Private Hotel, in Bali also, and is due for completion late-2012. Shortly after, further Luna2 Private Hotels, each with adjacent Luna2 studios, have been planned in key locations around the region by 2014.

Previously, Melanie grew up as an expatriate child in Africa and the Caribbean. She later returned to her home town in London, and soon after in 1987 worked for six years in management and visual merchandising at the renowned Knightsbridge department store, Harrods. She later moved in 1993 to become the UK Head of Visual Merchandising for Polo Ralph Lauren. From there, in 1996, sh became the Asia Pacific Head of Creative for Calvin Klein Asia, based in Hong Kong. She is married with three children.

MET Studio

Add: 6 Maidstone Building Mews, 72-76 Borough High Street, London SE1 1GD, UK
Tel: +44 20 7378 7348; Fax: +44 20 7378 7330
Web: www.metstudio.com

MET Studio was originally set up in 1982 by its Chairman and founder Alex McCuaig, taking its name from the Metropolitan Wharf in London, where the company's first design studio was sited. Twenty-seven years later, the company enjoys a global reputation, with a lengthy list of highly-acclaimed masterplanning, museum, exhibition, visitor centre, zoo, special event, retail, AV and branding projects, created for corporate clients such as Cunard, De Beer, Virgin, Lucent, Swire, Hongkong Telecom, Portugal Telecom and The Wellcome Trust, as well as noncorporate clients including The Dutch, Irish and Macau Governments, the local councils of Hull and Birmingham and the London Borough of Southwark, as well many national museums around the world.
MET Studio has won some of the world's most prestigious business and design awards, including The Queen's Award for Enterprise and the Business Link Exporter of the Year Award, as well as being a winner at The Museum of the Year Awards, The DBA Design Effectiveness Awards (which measure the tangible results of design) and taking Design Week's top plaudit – the Best of Show Award – for the best design of any kind in a twelve month period. The company has offices in London and Hong Kong.

Michel Penneman

Add: 3, avenue Macau B-1050 Brussels
Tel: +32 2 649 19 11
Web: www.michelpenneman.com

Michel Penneman graduated in architectural drawing from the Institut Saint-Luc in Brussels. He started his career in 1986 in the Tractebel consultancy, then became a CAD consultant for several major architectural firms in 1988. In July 1994, he created his own company, Détrois SA, specialised in creating architectural computer-generated imagery.
Parallel to Détrois, he did interior designs such as the Antoine Camus jewellery shop in Paris, the Hall of Time watch shop at the Conrad Hotel Brussels, and hotels like Tenboshhouse, the Vintagehotel and the White Hotel in Brussels. Michel Penneman is continually searching for original concepts. His key words are quick execution, low price, and high-quality lighting and acoustics.

MIEL Architects

Tel: 0034 93 245 62 19
Email: info@mielarquitectos.com
Web: www.mielarquitectos.com

MIEL Architects is the studio founded by Miguel Angel Borrás and Elodie Grammont. Based in Barcelona, they have been developing projects of architecture since 2001.MIEL Architects are focused in interior renovation and refurbishment, where acting in existing buildings allows them to discover and give voice to its remaining energies, beginning a dialogue with new needs and stopping their entropy by discovering new ways of experiencing them.

Modo Design

Add: 39 w 19th street, suite# 603 New York, NY 10011, USA
Tel: 212.924.7589
Web: www.mododesignNYC.com

Modo Design was founded in 2004 as a multidisciplinary architecture and interior design studio. Based in New York City, their main goal is client satisfaction through the conceptualisation and creation of interior and exterior spaces. They have done it successfully locally and internationally.
With passion and knowledge, their team works in full collaboration with their clients to find the right answer for each one of the projects.
They know that every client is different and they embrace their individuality with their personalised and custom design services, to fulfill the most minimum detail in their wish lists and always with careful consideration of the client's budget and schedule.
In their constant search for the best solutions to their projects, they recently became LEED Certified, to better serve their clientele and make sure they respond to their clients' inquiring minds with the knowledge and experience necessary. At Modo Design, they are in business to help their clients achieve what matters to them. Their projects reflect their client's goals, ideals, lifestyles, personalities and core values.

MoHen Design International

Add: No 18, Alley 396 Wulumuqi South Road, 200031 Shanghai, China
Tel: 8621-64370910; Fax: 8621-64317125
Web: www.mohen-design.com

Mohen Design International is an award-winning company creating schemes for residential, contract, office and hospitality design in Shanghai, Chongqing, Tokyo and Taiwan. The practice was initially set up by Mr. Hank M. Chao as a platform for cross-disciplinary collaborations. Today the German, Spanish, American, Japanese, Australian, Taiwanese and Chinese press has reviewed the practice's work. Mohen Design International projects range from public buildings to individual interiors for private clients. The practice has particular experience in the leisure and hospitality industry and developers, focusing on the design of contemporary bars, clubs and restaurants, hotels and private villas. Using a unique language of colour, light and geometry, their interiors are sensuous and eventful. Space is carefully choreographed into stylish environments.
Each design is treated individually and developed with the help of specialist consultants. Traditional architectural services are complemented with concept and brand development. Established contacts to graphic designers, photographers, media consultants, individual artists offer extended interdisciplinary support.

Montalba Architects, Inc.

Add: 2525 Michigan Avenue, Bldg. T4, Santa Monica, CA 90404, USA
Tel: +1 310 828 1100; Fax: +1 310 828 1162
Web: www.montalbaarchitects.com

Montalba Architects, Inc. is an award-winning practice, producing selected architecture and urban design related projects in the United States, Europe, and the Middle East. By embracing a humanistic approach that considers not only a client's needs and site considerations, but also the cultural and economic environment, solutions realised are contextual, yet conceptual and visionary in their intent, effect, and appeal. Projects emphasise conceptual experiences by creating environments that are both socially responsive and aesthetically progressive. The forces of volumetric landscapes, material integrity, the sculpting of natural light, as well as the purity of spatial volumes create solutions to pragmatic requirements of the client, constructability, and context. The depth of its award-winning portfolio highlights Montalba Architects' emphasis on design-oriented practice.
Montalba Architects has compiled an acclaimed and diverse collection of projects ranging in scale from commercial office interiors to residential homes, retail stores to mixed-use buildings and master planning.

Mr. Important Design

Add: 3748 Enos Avenue, Oakland, CA 94619, USA
Tel: (415) 573-9840
Web: www.misterimportant.com

Mr. Important Design is an interior design firm that brings an ebullient perspective to interiors. Specialising in nightclubs, restaurants, bars and lounges, as well as select residential and retail projects, Mr. Important Design works closely with clients to achieve interiors that exceed expectations – exuberant interiors that are designed to be remembered and talked about.
Collaboration with emerging designers and artists worldwide keeps the work fresh and surprising. Use of cutting edge technologies in lighting and materials coupled with a deep background in traditional furniture and décor help produce the unexpected thrill of these spaces. Founded in 2005 by Charles Doell, the firm's works have been widely featured in international publications. Wallpaper* Magazine has dubbed Charles Doell as a design whiz-kid.

NAÇO Architecture

Add: 66, BD DIDEROT, 75012 Paris, France
Tel. +33 (0)1 4345 0666; Fax. +33 (0)1 4307 2777
Web: www.naco.net

Since the creation of NAÇO Paris in 1991, his founder, the architect Marcelo Joulia knew and decided that architecture would not be the only ground of adventure in the agency but to compose their global environment" its spaces, volumes and signs – architecture, interior design, design, graphic, image, multimedia, fashion, events, scenography, and etc.
NAÇO's design is articulated on the real control of new technologies with an important part of their activity exclusively dedicated to research in exploring new boundaries.

Nendo

Add: 2-2-16-5F Shimomeguro Meguro-ku, Tokyo, 153-0064 Japan
Tel:+81-(0)3-6661-3750 Fax:+81-(0)3-6661-3751
Web: www.nendo.jp

Oki Sato was born in Toronto, Canada in 1977. He achieved M.A. in Architecture from Waseda University, Tokyo and established Nendo Tokyo office in 2002. In 2005, Oki Sato established the Nendo Milan office. He lectured for Showa Women's University in 2006 and Kuwasawa Design School in 2009, and published Ghost Stories in 2010. Nendo achieved The 100 Most Respected Japanese in 2006 and The Top 100 Small Japanese Companies in 2007.
Oki Sato's private exhibitions include: "Bloomroom" Milan Design Week in 2005; "Elastic Diamond" Milan Design Week, "Kuuki" Le Bain gallery in 2008; "Ghost stories" Friedman Benda gallery, "Ghost Stories" Museum of Arts and Design in 2009; "Chair Garden" Antonia Jannone Gallery in 2010.

ONG&ONG Pte Ltd.

Add: 510 Thomson Road, SLF Building #11-00, Singapore 298135
Tel: +65 6258 8666; Fax: +65 6259 8648
Web: www.ong-ong.com

Founding partners, the late Mr. Ong Teng Cheong and Mrs. Ong Siew May, established Ong & Ong Architects in 1972. Since its humble beginnings, the firms' staff strength has grown to almost 500 over the past four decades. Going from strength to strength under robust and exceptional leadership, the organisation was incorporated in 1992.
With a track record of almost 40 years in the industry, ONG&ONG has earned an unparalleled reputation for integrating skilled architecture, clever interior design, creative environmental branding and sensitive landscape design. Paramount to their success lies in their insistence on servicing their clients with creativity, excellence and commitment. They continually strive to uphold their mission to be the designer of their age – a premier design practice both locally and in the region.
Partnering their clients in their race to the top, ONG&ONG now offers a complete 360° solution – i.e. a parceled cross-discipline integrated solution, encompassing all aspects of the construction business. In addition to projects in Singapore, ONG&ONG has also completed large-scale developments regionally. This has prompted the setting up of offices in China, Vietnam, India and Malaysia. In-depth knowledge of the local context, culture and regulations allow them to better understand their clients' needs. They are an ISO14001 certified practice and consistently strive to meet and exceed their clients' expectations. To grow their international reputation, ONG&ONG has now set up an office in New York, USA.

Outline

Add: 10 Stoney street London SE1 9AD, UK
Tel: 020 7378 1616, Fax: 020 8378 8366
Web: http://www.outline-projects.co.uk

Michael Westthorp graduated from the Royal College of Art and went to work for several leading architecture and interior design practices before establishing Outline in 2001. From their offices in Borough Market London, Outline has gone on to be a widely published and award-winning practice, working across the fields of hospitality, retail and housing. Michael strongly believes in collaboration as a creatively productive tool and as such, works with a network of contractors, craftsmen, consultants and artists to deliver innovative design led spaces. They work most closely with their clients, exploring the concept's potential by creating identity through interiors. Outline is currently working on retail and restaurant projects in and around London.

PAL Design Consultants Ltd.

Add: 29/F, Chinachem Leighton Plaza, 29 Leighton Road, Causeway Bay, Hong Kong
Tel. 852 2877 1233; Fax. 852 2824 9275
Web: www.paldesign.cn

Born in Hong Kong, as Hong Kong top ten designer and the founder and principal designer of PAL Design Consultants Ltd., Patrick Leung is well-known designer for international awards winner. Sharp on three-dimensional space design, he is excellent in creative and innovative design that blends east and west culture, and between the modern and classic. Its space emphasises on timeless, tasteful creativity and comfort.
At 1978, he graduated in design with distinction from the Polytechnic University and started his career in interior design. In 1994, he established his own firm PAL Design Consultants Ltd. He and his studio has won more than 50 international awards. The most outstanding one is the IFI Grand Prize Design Award at 2007 presented by IFI (International Federation of Interior Architects / Designers) honour to his project as one of the World Best Interior Design. In 2009, his project Doubletree by Hilton Beijing has awarded as Merit Award of Best of Year presented by Interior Design USA. His 3 projects have been selected by the judges for inclusion on shortlist of FX International Design Awards.
During 2008-2010, Patrick awards as Top 50 World's Leading Interior Designers of "Andrew Martin International Interior Design Awards", China Enterprise Awards for Creative Businessmen, The Influential Man of the Greater China Interior Designer Award, The Annual Most Influential Designer Award, Annual Outstanding Designer and China Top10 Grand Designer. He is appointed as Honorary Advisor of HKIDA and members of various Committees of HKTDC. He is also a Member of Spatial Arts and Design Committee of China Artist Association.

Panorama

Add: Unit 7B, Charmill Centre, 50 Hillwood Road, Tsimshatsui, Kowloon, Hong Kong
Tel: 852 2317 7850; Fax: 852 2317 7851
Web: www.panoramahk.com

As one of the most renowned Hong Kong interior designers in the recent decade, Horace Pan obtained his Bachelor of Arts degree in Interior Design and Master of Arts degree in Design from School of Design, The Hong Kong Polytechnic University. In 2003, he established his own interior & branding design practice PANORAMA.
The company has received a number of recognitions and awards over the years including the IDA Design Awards, JCD Design Awards Best 100, FRAME Great Indoors Awards Nominee, iF Design Awards China, China's Most Successful Design Awards, The Ring - iC@ward International Interior Design, Asia Pacific Interior Design Awards, Hong Kong Ten Outstanding Designers Award, Hong Kong Designers Association Awards, Perspective Design Recognition Awards and Design for Asia Awards Finalist. Projects have been featured in numerous international design magazines & journals, e.g. Netherland's FRAME, Japan's World Hyper Interiors, Singapore's ISH & d+a, Korea's Interior World & bob. Pan now furthers his professional career in the field of design education and is the assistant professor at School of Design, the Hong Kong Polytechnic University and serving as the Chairman of the Hong Kong Interior Design Association and the Director of Hong Kong Design Centre. He is frequently invited to be the guest speaker of international design conferences and seminars.

PARASITE Studio

Add: Str. LEV TOLSTOI, no. 16, TIMISOARA, Romania
Tel: 0040726311007, Fax: 004 0356818863
Web: http://www.parasitestudio.com

PARASITE signifies for them a change of attitude. It means to refer to the project from "above". They are interested in the conflict between old and new and not in the integration of the design through materials and details.
They believe that exactly this conflict could generate a different type of spatiality. They are not interested in the forms of "correct architecture" because they want to make a further leap. Architecture has to start to shape space in a different way, details must be seen in a contemporary fashion, they have to complete space instead of being the generators for architecture and theme.
The lack of details of the contemporary buildings must be understood as a change of architectural attitude, architecture has not grown poorer but has become something different.

Pascal Arquitectos

Add: Atlaltunco #99, Col. Lomas de Tecamachalco, CP 53970, Mexico D.F., Mexico
Tel: (5255) 5294-2371; Fax: (5255) 52948513
www.pascalarquitectos.com

The identity that supports the work developed by the firm, with headquarters in Mexico City since 1979, comes as a result from the fact that there is not an ulterior ideology normalising the form, the language or the materials used; the team work is aside from unique discourses ascribed to any project. For Pascal Arquitectos each practice, each work is the outcome of particular and determining factors such as available resources, social or location context, everything is exhaustively analysed. The commitment is at the same time with the client and the final user, as well with the environment and the city.
All the above is based upon an unique research process and experimentation using new materials and technologies. The atelier comprises a polyfunctional group whose development does not depends on typology specialisation that can become creativity and innovation restraint. For this reason at Pascal all kind of projects are produced: residential, corporate, contract and hospitality, temples or ritual spaces besides developing – depending on each particular case, the architecture, the interior and furniture design up to the lighting and landscape design too.
The work of the past thirty years have left a lot of knowledge and experience. Amongst the more representative are the Sheraton "Centro Histórico" hotel, located in front of the Alameda Central; and Meditation House, in Bosques de las Lomas, that has been internationally recognised with numerous awards. The atelier's work has been widely published.

Pericles Liatsos Designers

Add: Strovolos Park Building, 2a Elia Venezi Avenue Suite 401, 2042 Strovolos, Nicosia, Cyprus
Tel: +357 22 44 22 46; Fax: +357 22 44 22 47
Web: www.periclesliatsos.com

Pericles Liatsos Designers Ltd is a professional company established in 1999 offering a complete range of interior planning and design services as well as product design, focused on both residential and commercial spaces.
A staff of exceptional design talent has the experience of developing comprehensive interior planning for regional and international projects. They develop both Residential and Commercial design projects for their national and internationally based clientele, striving to provide truly innovative solutions and the highest quality range of services.
The office has designed a wide range of products for their clientele that includes furniture, bathroom and kitchen accessories, equipment and fittings as well as office accessories and lighting. The office has 7 interior designers, two 3d specialists and a product design section.
All personnel has degrees from the most famous design schools worldwide including Master Degree in Interior and Living Design at the Domus Academy Milan, BA in Interior Architecture London Metropolitan University, the Architectural Association School of Architecture, Interior Design at Manchester Metropolitan University, Master of Arts from Rome's Quassar in Interior Architecture, Master of Arts in Interior Design and Information Technology at UCE, UK to mention a few. Furthermore their office has its Marketing and Business Development department.

Philippe Starck

Add: 36 rue Scheffer, 75116 Paris, France
Tel: + 33 (0) 1 48 07 54 54, Fax:+ 33 (0) 1 48 07 54 64
Web: www.starck.com

Philippe Starck is an internationally acclaimed French creator, designer and architect. This tireless and rebellious citizen of the world who considers his duty to share his ethical and subversive vision of a fairer world, creates unconventional objects whose purpose is to be "good" before being beautiful. Most of his design has become cult objects and his hotels have become timeless icons and have added a new dimension to the global cityscape.
Being an enthusiastic advocate of sustainability, this "visionnaire" recently developed the revolutionary concept of "democratic ecology" by creating affordable wind turbines for the home, soon to be followed innovative prefab ecological wooden houses and solar boats. He lives, with his wife Jasmine, mostly on the airplane and in Paris, Burano, and his oyster farm in the Southwest of France.

PT Green Design

Add: Jalan Nangka SS Denpasar, Bali, Indonesia
Tel: 0062 81236795887
Email: ptgreendesign@hotmail.com

Giovanni D'Ambrosio was born in Rome on 5 July 1959. He had an artistic background, having studied advertising graphics and architecture in Rome; where his professional activity started. He started his activity as industrial designer showing at the 1995 International Furniture Design (Salone International del Mobile) in Milan. In the same year he was spotted on the map of the Young Italian Designers, published on the magazine Abitare (No.344). He is a member of ADI- The Italian Association for Industrial Design, and from 1994 he was made member of the Italian Superior Council of the National Institute of Architecture: IN/ARCH.
He won the first prize for the ENIT Italian Pavilion, the national tourism agency in 1989. He obtained an honourable mention with his NORDICA exhibition in Munich- Germany, in the 1991 IN/ARCH prizes, and with his contribution to the Grado Zero di Architettura in Modena 1998. Moreover he won the first prize for the project Treparcheggidi scambio, Monti Tiburtini in 2001.

RSP Architects Planners & Engineers (PTE) Ltd.

Add: 15 Scotts Road #07-00, Thong Teck Building Singapore 228218
Tel: +65 6737 7544; Fax: +65 6733 9143
Web: www.rsp.com.sg

RSP started out as a small partnership, Raglan Squire and Partners in 1956. It has grown in scope and scale to become one of the largest and most established practices in Asia. RSP's strength lies in its total commitment to Excellence in Planning and Design and in the delivery of Quality Buildings and Projects. The approach is client-centred and collaborative.
The management is innovative, quality diven and highly professional, supported by staff that are talented and resourceful. Together, the team builds upon RSP's brand and varied experience to offer clients a fully integrated multi-disciplinary professional service that is in a league of its own. With associated companies Squire Mech Pte Ltd (mechanical & electrical) and RSP Interiors Pte Ltd, the RSP Group has combined staff strength of about 1000, which includes eminent persons in senior management who are captains of the industry.

RTKL Associates Inc.

Add: 2101 L Street NW, Ste. 200, Washington DC 20037, USA
Tel: 202.912.8178; Fax: 202.887.5168
Web: www.rtkl.com

RTKL is a global architecture, engineering and planning design firm. Part of the ARCADIS global network since 2007, RTKL specializes in providing its multidisciplinary services across the full development cycle to create places of distinction and designs of lasting value. RTKL works with commercial, workplace, public and healthcare clients on projects around the globe.

SAKO Architects

Address: 1803,1801 Tower8, JianWai SOHO NO.39, East Third Ring Road, Chaoyang District, 100022 Beijing, China.
Tel: +86-10-5869-0901; Fax: +86-10-5869-1317
Web: www.sako.co.jp

Born in Fukuoka, Japan, as the principal of the firm, Keiichiro Sako was invited to work as visiting Scholar at Columbia University from 2004 to 2005. He established SAKO Architects and jointly presided over Asian Architects Associates in 2004.
They created numerous works including JEANSWEST in Suzhou, ROMANTICISM 3 in Hangzhou, STEPS in Beijing, GOBI in Ulaanbaatar, EIFINI2 in Chengdu, KID'S REPUBLIC4 in Shanghai, FLATFLAT in Harajuku, EIFINI in Beijing, BRANCH in Changchun, MOSAIC in Beijing, LATTICE in Beijing, STRIPES in Jinan, BEANS in Kanazawa, T in Tokyo, and so on.
Their works won many awards such as "JCD Design Award 2008 (Japan)"; "Silver Award of Romanticism2 in Hangzhou"; "Interior Design Award in China 2007"; "The 5th Modern Decoration International Media Prize (China)"; "Annual Best Designer"; "Innovational Top 10 on Tenment Design 2007 (China)"; "Gold Award" of BUMPS in Beijing; "science & technology Award 2007 (China)"; "Gold Award" of BUMPS in Beijing; "JCD Design Award 2007 (Japan)"; "Bronze Award" of Romanticism in Hangzhou; "Asian Apartment Award 2006 (China)", and so on.

Saunders Architecture

Add: Vestre Torggate 22m, 5015 Bergen, Norway
Tel: T +47 55 36 85 06, +47 97 52 57 61
Web: http://www.saunders.no

Saunders Architecture is a firm owned by Canadian Todd Saunders (born 1969 in Gander, Newfoundland) who has lived and worked in Bergen, Norway since 1997.
Saunders has worked in countries such Austria, Germany, Russia, and Latvia. Currently, the office is working mostly in Norway, and has projects in England, Denmark, Sweden, and Canada. The work of Saunders Architecture has been published in newspapers, magazines, and books worldwide.
Todd Saunders received a Bachelor of Environmental Planning & Design from the Nova Scotia College of Art and Design, Halifax, Canada. While doing his bachelors, Saunders spent a semester as an exchange student at the Rhode Island School of Design, Department of Architecture.
He subsequently received a Masters of Architecture from McGill University, Montreal, Canada. Saunders has been a part-time teacher at the Bergen Architecture School since 2001.
He has lectured at various architecture and design schools in Canada and England. In the spring of 2006, Saunders was a visiting professor at The University of Québec in Montreal, Canada.

SB Architects

Add: San Francisco, California One Beach Street,
Suite 301 San Francisco, CA 94133, USA
Tel: (415) 673-8990
Web: www.sb-architects.com

In five decades of practice, SB Architects has established a worldwide reputation for excellence in the planning and design of large scale hotel, resort, vacation ownership, multi-family residential and mixed-use projects. Widely recognized for their highly individual approach to design, the firm has received over 200 awards for design excellence.
With a staff of highly trained, immensely talented and deeply passionate individuals in their San Francisco and Miami offices, SB Architects successfully merged fifty years of experience with the energy, drive and dedication of their second generation of partners.
With the technical capabilities and the understanding to take even the largest projects from initial concept through construction anywhere in the world, SB Architects remains a hands-on, design oriented practice at heart.
Integrity in design, connection to the client and balance in their corporate culture are integral to SB Architects' identity.

Simone Micheli Architect

Add: Via Aretina, 197r/199r/201r, 50136 Firenze, Italy
Tel:+39 055 69 12 16 Fax: +39 055 65 044 98
Web: www.simonemicheli.com

Simone Micheli founded the architectural studio having his name in 1990 and the Design Company named "Simone Micheli Architectural Hero" in 2003. Professor at the University, in particular at the Polidesign in Milan, at the Scuola Politecnica di Design in Milan. All the works by Architect Simone Micheli are unique and feature a strong personality in addition to being sustainable, environmental friendly. He plays a crucial role in the planning field in Europe, in fact he developed a number of plans for public administration and for prestigious customers related to the community and to the residence field.
A number of monographs and international magazines focused on his works are available. He exhibited his works at the Venice Biennale, in the architectural sector. He works as editor of the theme exhibition named "contract" as well of the major international exhibitions in this field. The planning company Simone Micheli Architectural Hero based in Florence and Milan provides contract and residence related services in different fields: architecture, interior design, design, visual design e communication.

Single Speed Design

Add: SsD NY, 325 West 38th Street, Suite 210, New York, USA
Tel: 212. 248. 7500; Fax: 866. 677. 3878
Web: www.ssdarchitecture.com

The work of SsD explores a version of sustainability that approaches design as a convergent, interdisciplinary, and collaborative venture. In this light, an economy of means is favored over an additive and redundant methodology: Instead of separating aspects of architecture, landscape, history, social systems, and codes into their constituent disciplines, these agendas are simultaneously explored so that minimum form can take maximum effect. Because this approach is inherently based on finding solutions that minimise material and energy use while maximising performance, sustainability emerges as an integrated result.
Along with being published in major media such as Metropolis Magazine, Dwell Magazine, The New Yorker, and PBS, SsD has received many prestigious design awards including the AIA Young Architects Award (2006 and 2009), the Young Architects Forum Award by the Architectural League of NY (2007), the Holcim Foundation for Sustainable Construction Award (2005), The Metropolis Next Generation Prize (2004), and six AIA awards (2003-2006). They have lectured and exhibited at many universities and conferences including venues at the Harvard GSD, Ohio State University, and Seoul National University, as well as at several national design conferences. SsD is a certified Minority and Woman owned business.

Six Senses

Add: 19/F Two Pacific Place Bui lding, 142 Sukhumvit Road, Klongtoey, Bangkok 10110, Thailand
Tel: +66 (0) 2631 9777; Fax: +66 (0) 2631 9799
Web: www.sixsenses.com

Six Senses is a resort and spa management and development company, established in 1995, which manages resorts under the brand names Soneva, Six Senses Hideaway and Evason, plus Six Senses Spas and Six Senses Destination Spas.

Slade Architecture

Add: 77 Chambers Street, 5th fl. New York, New York 10007, USA
Tel: 212 677 6380 Fax: 212 677 6330
Web: www.sladearch.com

Slade Architecture is a New York City based architecture and design firm founded in 2002 by James and Hayes Slade. The firm has completed a diverse range of domestic and international projects. Their work has been exhibited and published widely in over 200 publications. The Architecture League of New York selected Slade Architecture for the 2010 Emerging Voices Lecture Series held in the New Museum.
Among Slade Architecture's awards are a national AIA Small Projects Award, multiple NY AIA Merit Awards, Association of Retail Environments Store of the Year Award, Chain Store Age Best in Show Award, Fast Company Masters of Design issue, multiple Best of Year awards from Interior Design Magazine, Contract Magazine and Businessweek/Architectural Record.
Slade Architecture's work has been exhibited at the AIA Center for Architecture in New York, the Venice Biennale, Florida International University, the German Architecture Museum in Frankfurt and many other exhibits in Europe, Asia and the United States.

Squillace Nicholas Architects

Add: SNA Sydney 2 Liverpool Lane East Sydney NSW 2010, Australia
Tel: 61 2 8354 1300; Fax: 61 2 8354 1311
Web: www.squillacenicholas.com.au

SNA brings together the combined experience of architects Vince Squillace and Patrick Nicholas and the Sydney and Melbourne architectural and interior design teams. SNA has specialist expertise in the fields of single dwelling, medium density and high rise residential, hospitality, heritage, commercial, mixed use and sustainable design. They believe the experience of architecture is heightened through a building's engagement with landscape and climate, the interplay of light, and the sensuality of materials.

Stanley Saitowitz Natoma Architects

Add: 1022 Natoma Street, Unit 3, San Francisco, CA, USA
Tel: 415-626-8977; Fax: 415-626-8978
Web: http://www.saitowitz.com/

Stanley Saitowitz Natoma Architects Inc. is committed to design excellence. The theoretical position establishes a particular concept for each project, giving unique measure to the specific program and site. The approach to design is considered human geography, and is especially indicative of the relation of building and setting. The aim is to invent spaces of passionate quality.
Stanley Saitowitz is Professor Emeritus Of Architecture at the University of California, Berkeley, and has taught at a number of schools including the GSD, Harvard University (Eliot Noyes Professor 1991/2), University of Okalahoma (Bruce Goff Professor, 1993), Southern California Institute of Architecture, UCLA, the University of Texas, the University of the Witwatersrand, Cornell, and Syracuse. He has lectured extensively in the USA and internationally.

Studio 63 Architecture + Design

Add: Via Santo Spirito 6, Firenze 50125, Italy
Tel: +39 055 2399252
Web: Www.Studio63.It

Studio 63 Architecture + Design is based in the historical center of Florence Italy. The fruitful encounter between Piero Angelo Orecchioni and Massimo Dei led to the foundation of Studio 63 in 1998. By 2003, Studio 63 inaugurated its New York City office, by 2005 its office in Hong Kong and by 2008 its office in Shanghai and an operative partnership in Dubai.
Their creative team is composed of gifted professionals, coming from various disciplines, working together in a fertile and challenging multicultural exchange. A strong identity is the hallmark of their projects. This identity is the result of extended research, creative proposals and deep respect of the contemporary language criteria.
Studio 63 is operating in more than 25 countries around the world managing to the last detail projects from concept development through design and planning towards their complete achievement. Their specialties are retail design and hotelier.

Studio Arne Quinze

Add: SAQ Brussels Arenbergstraat 44, 1000 Brussels, Belgium
Tel: +32 23 005 910; Fax: +32 23 005 919
Web: http://www.saq.eu

SAQ is a conceptual and interdisciplinary design agency specializsd in developing spatial sceneries and concepts. The practice relies

on a broad range of competencies where both architects, interior designers, urbanists, video-artists and graphic designers team up according to the specific orientation or necessities of each project. SAQ believes strongly in co-operation and regularly invites professional experts or companies to participate in the materialization or the elaboration of an idea.
In this versatility, every project or concept undertaken by SAQ thrives to deliver to its end-user powerful and moving experiences where all senses can be stimulated and where the materialized space almost forms an event in itself. As long as there is a creation of sense.
SAQ considers the relationship with the client as a vital element in the design process. A successful project is always the fruit of passionate and constructive debates between client and studio. With as ultimate goal the satisfaction of the end-user. Currently, SAQ is also engaged in the master plan outline for mixed use development in Brussels and Berlin where the offices are equally located.

Studio Arthur Casas

Add: Rua Itápolis, 818 São Paulo Sp 01245 000, Brasil
Tel: + 55 11 2182 7500; Fax: + 55 11 3663 6540
Web: www.arthurcasas.com

As the founder of the firm, Arthur Casas graduated in 1983 from Mackenzie University in Sao Paulo with a degree in Architecture His architectural designs cover a scope of interior, residential, commercial and new construction projects.
Arthur Casas has claimed prestigious awards since the beginning of his career. Awards include: the 1989 Design Prize from the Casa Brasileira Museum; the A&D Magazine first prize in 1994; the 1997 Deca Prize for Bathrooms; and either first or second honors with Espaco D Magazine from 1998 to 2006 for his interior design, commercial ambiences and residential projects. In the year 2000, Interior Design awarded him first prize for Best City Hotel USA, and has since placed 20th for the Interior Design Hall of Fame for his furniture designs, residential projects and bathroom projects. In 2004, the IAB Institute and the 3rd Architecture Caue Award honoured Casas for his Ornare Store project.

Studiounodesign

Add: Pontedera Pisa, Italy
Email: info@studiounodesign.com
Web: www.studiounodesign.com

Studiounodesign was born from the collaboration between GABRIELE BARTOLOMEO and SIMONE NUTI with the intention of offering innovating and original ideas without risking the unfavourable reaction from customers and their requirements. Studiounodesign's target is the valorisation of the spaces and forms to reach a harmonious ambience.
Studiounodesign uses advanced technical resources that enables amazing achievements due to the endless dialogue between the two designers, and with the customer. Earnestness, professionalism, attention to details at every step of the project and freshness of ideas and proposals are characterise this firm.

Tham & Videgård Arkitekter

Add:Blekingegatan46, 11662 Stockholm, Sweden
Tel:+46 08 702 00 46 Fax: +46 08 702 00 56
Web: www.tvark.se

Tham & Videgård Arkitekter is a progressive and contemporary practice that focuses on architecture and design – from large scale urban planning through to buildings, interiors and objects. The practice objective is to create a distinct and relevant architecture with the starting point resting within the unique context and specific conditions of the individual project.
Taking an active approach, the office is involved throughout the whole process, from developing the early sketch to the on-site supervision. Commissions include public, commercial and private clients, in Sweden and abroad. The practice approach to architecture is inclusive; with practical, theoretical, social and environmental issues analysed and integrated within the process. When required and relevant the office involves a network of multidisciplinary external consultants. This use of complementing resources ensures that all projects address the right challenges, in order to make the most of the opportunities that each represent. Within the office architects combine straight forward solutions with extensive research.
From working with and completing several public, educational, exhibition and commercial buildings, the T&V team is experienced in managing projects that comply with the highest international standards regarding climate, security and long term sustainability. T&V are based in Stockholm, Sweden, and directed by co-founders and chief architects Bolle Tham and Martin Videgård.

Tighe Architecture

Add: 1632 Ocean Park Blvd Santa Monica, CA, USA
Tel: 310 450 8823; Fax: 310 450 8273
Web: www.tighearchitecture.com

Tighe Architecture is committed to creating an authentic, contemporary Architecture informed by technology, sustainability and building innovation.
The work is not of style but of process, a process driven by influences such as site, environment, budget, society, and culture. Since the inception of Tighe Architecture, a strong and diverse body of projects has been realized including city developed affordable housing.
Commercial and mixed use projects, civic art, installations and residences. The firm advocates a collaborative approach and has developed an extensive network of highly skilled consultants, artisans, and trades people.
Sustainability is an integral component in all the work as evidenced by The Sierra Bonita Mixed use affordable Housing project for people living with disabilities. The building is now under construction and serves as a pilot for the City of West Hollywood's newly implemented Green Building Ordinance.
Recently, Patrick Tighe Architecture completed the US headquarters for the UK based Moving Picture company. (a division of Technicolour) located in downtown Santa Monica. Projects are now in development in Morocco, Asia and the Middle East.

Trustindesign

Add: Trustindesign 5, rue du Pasteur Wagner, 75011 Paris, France
Tel / Fax: +33 (0)9 50 19 03 58
Web: www.trustindesign.com

Established in 2004 by Joran Briand, Etienne Vallet and Arthur de Chatelperron, it marks the beginning of a prolific and innovative collaboration. Trustindesign is an interdisciplinary studio involving architecture, interior, graphic and product design.
The studio is interested in the emerging relationships across different design disciplines and in the opportunities offered to designers by technological innovation.
With collaborators specializing in different areas, each project is developed with an integral approach that challenges preconceptions and seeks alternative ways of living. Trustindesign is a collaboration that emerges from the awareness of the complexity of their world and attempts to make sense of it through the lenses of design.

TWS & Partners

Add: Wisma 21, Jl. Kembang Permai Raya Blok 1-4 No.3, Puri Indah, Kembangan Selatan, Jakarta 11610, Indonesia.
Tel: 62 21 582 8086; Fax:62 21 582 8427
Web: www.twspartners.com

As the principal of TWS & Partners, Tonny Wirawan Suriadjaja was born on 30 January 1972, Jakarta, Indonesia, Tonny Wirawan Suriadjaja is an architect who always tries to find any innovation in architectural and design interior.
His fields is ranging from urban scale to products, interior and furniture. He always tries to discover something new that can improve his design and products. During 1990 and 1995, Tonny studied architecture at Tarumanegara University. In 1995 he worked with Mr. Gunawan Tiahjono Ph.d to design the National Museum in Korea. In the same year, he joined Shimizu Lampiri Consultant. Tonny worked in Ciputra Development from 1995 to 1998. He has been worked as the principal at TWS & Partners since 1998.

UXUS

Add: Keizersgracht 174, 1016 DW Amsterdam, the Netherlands
Tel: +31 20 623 3114
Web: http://www.uxusdesign.com

UXUS is an international multidisciplinary creative company founded in 2003, from the shared creative vision of three passionate and dynamic individuals. With offices in the US and Europe, their international team integrates the diverse design needs of many cultures. UXUS provides design services across the entire spectrum of interiors, architecture, hospitality, retail, identity, graphics and packaging.
Their multi-disciplinary structure, with teams from different disciplines working together, promotes a culture of interchange and adds tremendous value to the creative process and final result. UXUS offers a full service, from concept through completion, tailored to your specific requirements.
All of their clients benefit from their world-class resources and international network of collaborators ensuring the highest level of execution possible. Among their clients are, Nokia, Levi's, Heineken, McDonald's, Nespresso, Tate Modern, Adidas, Rijksmuseum to name a few. UXUS is an internationally recognized design agency that has received world-class recognition by the press and international award committees.

Wunderteam.pl

Tel: +48 663 732 443
Web: www.wunderteam.pl

Paulina Stepien, Magdalena Piwowar – they joined forces in 2008 creating a design duo called Wunderteam.pl. Since then, they grew into real wunderteam, because now our team consists of 3 people. They have been working on interiors of public utility buildings, including historic structures and furniture design but also fashion design projects. This wide scope of projects has been a well considered decision. The diversity in design issues entails an enrichment of any project. Their team switches easily from innovative solutions to the principles of ergonomics and usability. They design interiors of public utility buildings, including historic structures, but they also do furniture and fashion design.
Their inspiration comes from space where architecture blends with art and design and combines functionalism, technical knowledge and creativity. Their clients mainly are public institutions, developers, and private clients. Their main goal is to create inspiring interiors and products that enhance life at large. A surrounding in which people can live and work in an optimized way and where the investments made are fully effected.

XTEN Architecture

Add: 10315 Jefferson Boulevard, Culver City, California 90232, USA
Tel: 310-773-4188; Fax: 310-287-2002
Web: www.xtenarchitecture.com

XTEN Architecture is an award-winning architecture firm located in Los Angeles, California, with associate offices near Basel, Switzerland.
Founded in 2000 by partners Monika Häfelfinger and Austin Kelly AIA, LEED AP, XTEN Architecture is a full service architecture and design firm specializing in cultural buildings, office and commercial facilities and residential estates. Building designs are developed using innovative materials and sustainable technologies, and guided from schematic design through construction. XTEN approaches architecture with an emphasis on minimalist logic, material transformation and refined detailing and craftsmanship. The architects develop strong sculptural forms and open spaces transformed by direct connections to nature. XTEN Architecture has been awarded the International Architecture Award from the Chicago Athenaeum and European Centre for Architecture, the American Architecture Award, the IV Miami + Design Biennal Architecture Award, the AIA California Council Architecture Award, and several Design Awards from the American Institute of Architects.
The firm's work has been published in books and magazines internationally. XTEN projects are in design and construction in the United States, Switzerland, Asia and the Middle East.

HAUTE SPACES: RESIDENCES

Published in Asia in 2011 by
Page One Publishing Pte Ltd
20 Kaki Bukit View Kaki Bukit Techpark II
Singapore 415956
Tel: [65] 6742-2088
Fax: [65] 6744-2088
enquiries@pageonegroup.com
www.pageonegroup.com

First published 2011 by Dopress Books
No 85, Huanghe South Street,
110031 Shenyang, China
Tel: +86-24-88622666
Fax: +86-24-88680777
info@dopress.com
www.dopress.com

Page One design and editorial team: Rachel Koh, Stacy Tan

ISBN 978-981-428-627-5

Printed in China